Dot

QUEEN OF RIVERSTONE CASTLE

Dot

QUEEN OF RIVERSTONE CASTLE

RANDOM HOUSE
NEW ZEALAND

Dot Smith *with*
Nathalie Brown

A RANDOM HOUSE BOOK published by Random House New Zealand

18 Poland Road, Glenfield, Auckland, New Zealand

For more information about our titles go to www.randomhouse.co.nz

A catalogue record for this book is available from the National Library of New Zealand

Random House New Zealand is part of the Random House Group

New York London Sydney Auckland Delhi Johannesburg

First published 2014

ISBN 978 1 77553 543 0

eISBN 978 1 77553 544 7

Design: Megan van Staden

Cover photograph: Fiona Andersen

Printed in New Zealand by Printlink

This publication is printed on paper pulp sourced from sustainably grown and managed forests, using Elemental Chlorine Free (ECF) bleaching, and printed with 100% vegetable-based inks.

Contents

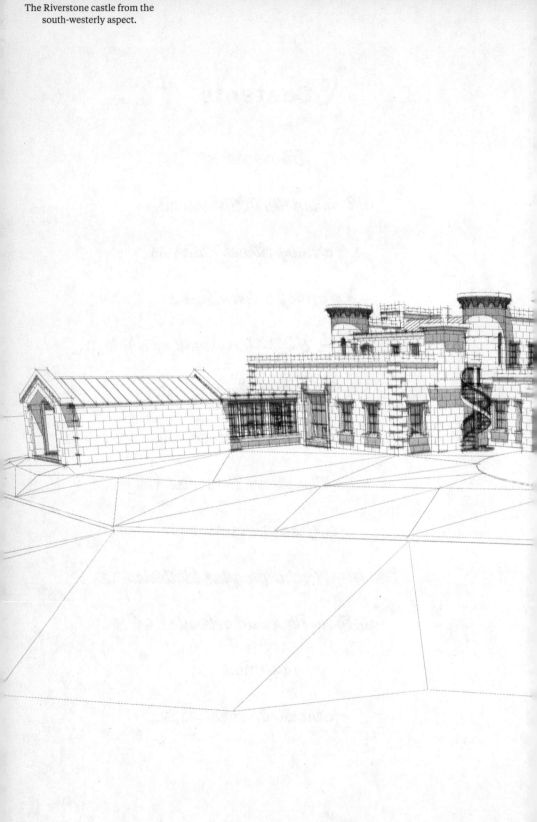

The Riverstone castle from the south-westerly aspect.

Foreword

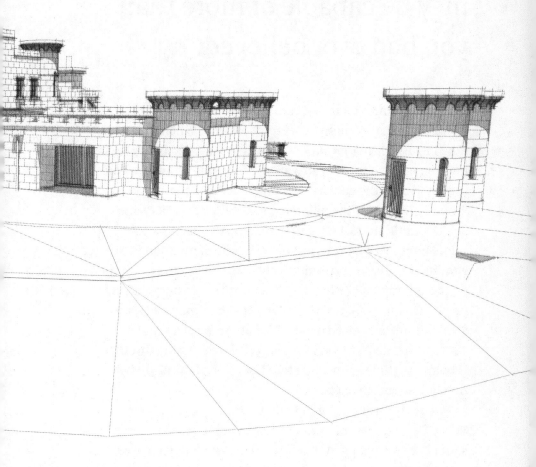

Take my word for it: Dot Smith can change your life. After spending just a few hours with her, you begin to see that you may be capable of more than you had ever believed.

My introduction to Dot came at seven o'clock on a Thursday evening in September 2009. When the phone rang I nearly didn't pick it up, because I assumed it would be my teenage son, too lazy to walk the four steps from the house to my office in the garage to tell me that dinner was ready. When I did answer the phone, this rather raspy voice said, 'It's Dot Smith here. I want to build a castle.' That's all she said. My immediate reaction was that one of my friends was winding me up, so very tentatively I said 'Yes?', and she went on to explain that she lived on a farm at Hilderthorpe, 12 km north of Oamaru. She'd been dreaming of living in a castle all of her life, and she'd been told that I was the architect who could help her. Then she asked if I was coming through Oamaru anytime soon, and I told her I was planning to be there in two or three weeks.

Two weeks went by and I hadn't done anything about it. When I got another phone call from Dot, I realised she was serious, so we arranged that I'd be there the following week.

Within minutes of meeting her, I had completely warmed to this tall, leggy woman with an infectious laugh and flamboyant streaks of pink highlighting her dark hair. She's forthright and direct, with unbelievable energy. The sheer force of her personality makes you think: 'Wow! This woman is awesome!' I came away from Oamaru so excited, not just because I was going to design a castle, but because I knew working with her was going to be a ball!

They don't do things by halves in the Smith family. Dot and her husband, Neil — known as 'Smithy' — have worked their way up from buying the poorest dairy farm in the Waitaki in the early 1980s, to the point where they now own six dairy farms in the district and produce more than a million kilograms of milk solids a year. Their elder son, Mike, is as masterful a dairy farmer as their younger son Bevan is a chef and restaurateur.

I hadn't heard of Riverstone Kitchen at the time. That was before they won the *Cuisine* magazine New Zealand Restaurant of the Year award in 2010 and were joint winner for the Best Casual Dining award in 2011. The restaurant is very upmarket, with expanses of polished concrete, glass and stainless steel — the diametrical opposite of Riverstone Country, Dot's large gift and homeware shops with their Wild West frontages, just a few steps away. The most frequent comment you'll hear from people browsing in this phantasmagoria is: 'How on *earth* does she do her stocktake?'

And then there are the gardens. While the restaurant was under construction, Dot and Bevan planted herbs and leafy greens in two raised beds measuring 40 m x 5 m, with an access path in the middle. When Riverstone Kitchen opened in 2006, the home-grown produce was a big feature of the menu. The *Cuisine* magazine awards in 2010/2011 brought a 50 per cent increase in patronage overnight, and it hasn't fallen since. They definitely needed more food for the restaurant, and Dot, as head gardener, established 24 more 4-sq-m raised garden beds beside the restaurant. Then there are the poultry runs, orchards, potagers, aviaries and playgrounds she has built. Altogether, the grounds cover well over a hectare. I am a passionate gardener myself, but when I walked around the gardens at Riverstone I was amazed at what she had achieved.

Dot's approach to life is that if you want something you just get out there and find a way to make it happen. She often says, 'If you can imagine it, you can do it.' Since knowing Dot, another friend and I have come up with a new saying whenever we want to achieve something: 'Think it, say it, do it.' And we're no longer amazed at how well it works.

Often Dot has a direct influence on the people around her. In the interests of gathering ideas for her castle grounds, she and I went on a bus tour of the great gardens of Britain with a group of New Zealand and Australian women aged 55-plus. Most of us were grey-haired — but not Dot, with her black curls and pink flourishes — and wore rather muted colours. By the end of the tour there were splashes of primary colours everywhere. Every woman on the bus had added something to her wardrobe — a bright orange scarf, a fresh pink blouse, a colourful brooch . . .

When Dot wants to do something, she doesn't spend time thinking about what anyone else might say, or consider the possibility that it might be too hard or too expensive. She just finds a way to make it happen. She doesn't go in for introspection. She doesn't analyse her responses and feelings, and she doesn't have the self-doubt that many of us indulge in. What's more, she doesn't let up on herself. She has all the classic signs of being a coeliac, with a lactose intolerance, and she has learnt to adapt her diet to treat the symptoms. Yet in all the overseas travelling I've done with her — three times to China and the garden tour of the UK — she has never complained about feeling ill; she has never made a fuss about special meals. She has had a bad back for decades and was given a brace to wear, but she said she couldn't milk the cows in it, so it has been lying in the bottom drawer of her dresser for the past 20 years. She just ignores the pain and does a lot of gardening on her knees.

On my first trip to Riverstone, Dot gave me a foolscap box — pink, of course — filled with pages pulled from magazines with photographs of interiors, exteriors and gardens; details she would like to see in and around her castle. I took it back to my office in Wanaka, and, as I went through the pages, I realised that some of them came from magazines published in the 1980s. She had been gathering ideas for her castle for 30 years!

I have designed two castles for Dot. The first one was to be a fairly modest construction on a separate property from the home farm, restaurant and shopping complex. Then, just as we had all the paperwork ready to apply for resource consent, Smithy came up with an alternative plan and we started the process again — this time bigger and more ambitious.

Dot has a great imagination, but she's also very practical. She's clear about what she likes and what she doesn't, so building the castle is an evolving process. We'll have something nailed down, then she'll see something else and say, 'Oh God! We could do that!' Right from the start I recognised that her instincts were good, and nine times out of 10 I just developed her thoughts, got them down on paper, and they worked.

Dot's castle should be complete, standing on its island, surrounded by a 3-m deep moat, in late 2014. Maybe a bit later. As I work my way through the project, I always keep in mind that Dot knows what she's doing. If she wants something done, my job is to make it happen. And enjoy the ride with her.

Sarah Scott
Registered Architect, FNZIA

Sarah Scott Architects Ltd
Wanaka

CHAPTER 1

Growing Up in Northland

In my mind I have always been a princess in a castle. In the 1950s, when I was a six-year-old growing up on a dairy farm north of Auckland, I imagined my life in a fairy-tale castle, running along secret passages and dreading what lay in the dungeons. For years I covered sheets of paper with drawings of the castle I would live in.

It had towers and turrets, a drawbridge and a moat. It never occurred to me that I might *not* live in a castle some day. After all, I always believed my Prince Charming would come and build one for me. And my father taught me that if I wanted to achieve something badly enough, and if I worked for it single-mindedly, then I was sure to succeed.

Fifty-nine years later, in September 2013, all of New Zealand was treated to a magnificent storm. There was thunder and lightning, tremendous 140 kph gales, torrents of rain. Trees were uprooted everywhere, and here in North Otago the wind huffed and puffed and blew my half-built castle down.

Most of the ground-floor walls had been erected and were scheduled to be completed within three days, at which time the men would come to pour the concrete into the blockwork cores. The engineer, Tim Bradford, wanted to make sure there were no 'cold joins' in the concrete, because these can weaken the structure. This meant that the walls had to be filled in one go, rather than as they went up. Most of the structure was braced, but the panels between the windows in the kitchen, the dining room and our bedroom weren't braced, because the blockies were still working on them.

By three in the afternoon, the unbraced castle walls were swaying 20 cm from the foundations, and the steel reinforcing was bent over from the top of the windows to the floor as if a giant crane had pulled it over. Ian Gold — 'Goldie' — and his blockies were running around with big timber braces, trying to hold the castle together. Then the wind blew in the four big panels between the windows' frames. I was in tears. 'Bugger! How can this be happening?'

Goldie was ashen. He looked as though there had been a death in the family. It was so frightening, but after the storm stopped raging and moved on it took them only two days to repair the damage, and then we were all laughing about it. My castle would survive and go on to be finished.

Let me take you back to how this dream of a castle came to be. I think it's fair to say that it all began with my father. He was Bernard Lindsay Worthington, known to everyone as 'Burn', and the youngest of six children. Dad was a man before his time, one who always did things bigger and better than anyone else. He had a hard upbringing. His father had a stroke while working on the farm, and died two or three years later of a heart attack. My grandmother found it hard to cope alone with such a large family and no breadwinner, so Dad, as an underprivileged child, was sent to Dilworth School in

Bernard Worthington, aged 14 at Dilworth School. Dad once got 30 canes across his arse for talking in prayers. He couldn't move or sit down for a week.

DILWORTH ULSTER INSTITUTE
GREAT SOUTH ROAD,
AUCKLAND,
N.Z.

27th August, 1920. *192__*

Mrs Worthington,

TAUMARANUI.

Madam,

Your letter applying for the withdrawal of your boy was placed before the Board at its last meeting and it was decided to return him to you, as you suggest, at the end of the year. I shall be glad if before the time comes for him to go home you will send such clothes as he will need to travel in as his school clothing must be left here.

Bernard has grown a great deal and improved in many ways since he has been here and in outside things he is very useful, but just because of this, I want to warn you against sending him to work before 1922 at the earliest. He is big for his age and on a farm would be expected to do more work than he really has strength for. This might do much harm. The Board therefore advises you to give him at least one year more at school after leaving the Institute.

I am glad to know that your own business has prospered so that you are now able to provide for him.

I am,

Yours faithfully,

Ned Gibson

Headmaster.

Auckland. His lasting memories of his school days were killing the sheep to provide meat for the school. He left school at the age of 14 to work in the bush at Taumarunui, and then moved to Wellsford in 1932 to take up farming.

This was at the height of the Great Depression, when most farmers were going broke and walking off the land, but Dad saw an opportunity where everyone else saw only hard graft and failure. He bought 600 acres of land that had been part of the kauri gum fields, and paid £1 an acre for the best of it.

The land Dad bought had heavy clay soils, bog holes and kauri stumps. The back paddock was a very steep hill that grew gorse and manuka. It was prone to slips, and no matter what Dad did to it over the years he could never grow grass there, so he called it Mount Misery. The farm had never been worked over, but his neighbour, a Mr Harmer, bred draught horses, and they came to an agreement that Dad would break the horses into plough chains for him in return for the use of the horsepower.

Soon he had an eight-horse team pulling a double plough, and he worked them with great skill. His two furrow horses were straight-walkers, and he had another horse to bring them around into the furrow. Until the early 1940s kauri gum was a valuable export commodity, used to make resin and varnish for furniture. In the early days there was still a little kauri gum left in the ploughed ground, and this gave Dad a modest amount of money to live on while he broke in the land.

Because he had not yet seeded pasture, he had to feed the horses by hand. And as there were no vets in the area, he learnt to treat any injuries to the horses with common sense and old home remedies. People in the district saw him as a great horseman who worked to his last ounce of strength, a no-nonsense man who said exactly what he meant. His only interests outside farming were gardening and playing football for the United Football Club, where he was also a vocal side-line referee.

Mum and Dad's wedding photo with Rosemary Whitmore as bridesmaid on the right.

Dad's brand-new slurry wagon as it arrived on the front lawn.

He also had an eye for a pretty, capable girl, and courted my mother, Nancy Atkinson, who lived just down the road. He'd been living in a little nikau hut but before they were married in 1937, Dad built a cottage for her. For the rest of her life Mum lived a quiet, homely existence and stoically accepted the hard work that women of her era had to deal with.

Dad used to plough with the big draught horses at night because he could get a lot more out of them in the cool of the evening than during the hot, humid days. He brought in all the land with his horses, which were replaced when tractors and other machinery became available. He still had a few draught horses in the paddock in the late 1950s, and used them for the very last time to plough a big stretch of ground in front of the house, which he and my mother filled with daffodils and jonquils. Then the old horses were sold off.

Dad was determined to succeed as a farmer, and was eventually milking 200 cows when everyone else had 35. He built himself a lime crusher, and was the first in the Wellsford district to quarry and spread lime on the land. He'd shovel the lime dust onto the back of the truck, put the truck in first gear, and let it crawl in a straight line while he stood on the back to shovel it off again onto the paddock. When he got to the end of a paddock, he'd jump down, get into the cab of the truck, turn it around and go back the other way.

The lime raised the pH levels in the soil and dealt to the acidity of the depleted kauri gum fields. It also increased the moisture retention of the hard clay and improved pasture growth. Dad got letters from the Ministry of Lands and Survey, as it was in those days, to ask how he was achieving the results he reported. It was unheard-of for that type of country to be growing such good grass.

Dad was also one of the first dairy farmers to use cow manure to fertilise his paddocks. When all the washings came off the yard, he'd send them down a chute straight into an old slurry wagon, and then the slurry went straight back on the farm so

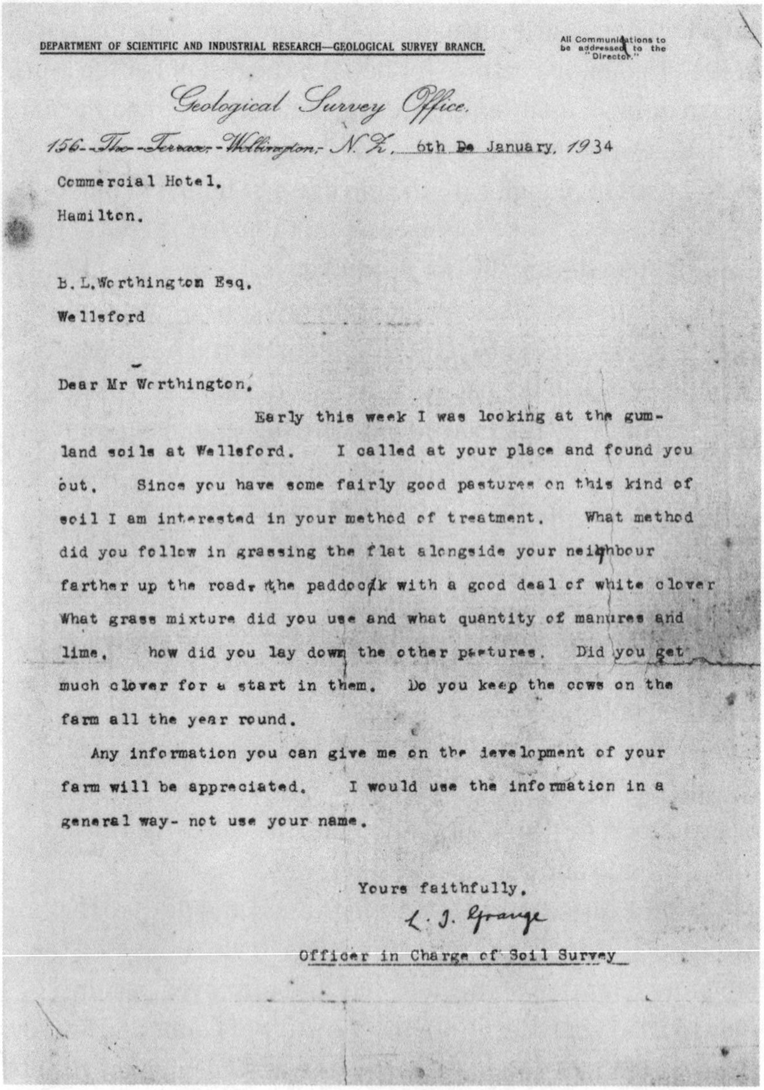

DEPARTMENT OF SCIENTIFIC AND INDUSTRIAL RESEARCH—GEOLOGICAL SURVEY BRANCH.

All Communications to
be addressed to the
"Director."

Geological Survey Office.

156 The Terrace Wellington, N.Z. 6th De January, 1934

Commercial Hotel,

Hamilton,

B.L.Worthington Esq.

Wellsford

Dear Mr Worthington,

Early this week I was looking at the gum-
land soils at Wellsford. I called at your place and found you
out. Since you have some fairly good pastures on this kind of
soil I am interested in your method of treatment. What method
did you follow in grassing the flat alongside your neighbour
farther up the road, the paddock with a good deal of white clover
What grass mixture did you use and what quantity of manures and
lime, how did you lay down the other pastures. Did you get
much clover for a start in them. Do you keep the cows on the
farm all the year round.

Any information you can give me on the development of your
farm will be appreciated. I would use the information in a
general way- not use your name.

Yours faithfully,

L. J. Grange

Officer in Charge of Soil Survey

A letter from Lands
& Survey, 1934.

that nothing was wasted. Everyone else sent it down the long drain — the nearest creek — and polluted the waterways. Even in the 1940s and 1950s, Dad knew it was a valuable soil nutrient and was determined not to waste it. These days all dairy farmers spread the effluent on their paddocks, and my gardens wouldn't be what they are today without it. It's liquid gold.

Then there was family life. Dad and Mum had five girls: Jenny, Judith, Patricia, Dorothy and Lyndsay. Jenny was born in 1939, nine years before me, so I barely knew her when I was a child. She was always slightly built, and loved gardening and horse riding. Cats, dogs and Goldie the horse would follow her up the creek when she was gathering blackberries. Because there were no boys in the family, Dad treated Jude as a tomboy and called her 'Johnny'. Eighteen months younger than Jenny, she was more interested in the farm than in school. Dad encouraged her to leave school at 15 so that she could work on the farm. Jude learnt to drive all the trucks and tractors, milk the cows, and did everything the men did. She went on to be a very successful businesswoman manufacturing high-quality workwear. She is also an intrepid traveller, and is a great gardener.

Pat was three years older than me. Tall, athletic and musical, she grew up to be a school teacher and taught kids from some of the poorest families in the North. She showed them how to grow vege gardens, and sold the produce to make money for the school. She bought a stove and had it installed into the classroom, then taught the kids to cook, getting the parents in to eat their cooking. This sort of thing is common now, but 45 years ago it was inspirational. In her home garden she grows plants from seeds and has taken cuttings all her life, as a true New Zealand-style gardener.

Lyn is two years younger than me and was my closest friend and companion until I moved to the South Island when I was in my thirties. She was the shortest of the girls, and had very curly hair. Mum used to twist it around her finger and give her a top-roll — much to her horror. When she left home, Lyn worked in the Westpac Bank. She is a mad keen gardener, and built a beautiful home on a man-made lake.

I was the fourth of the five Worthington daughters. Tall, sporty and always the clown, I laughed all day — I could laugh at nothing. Wave your finger, and I would laugh. Everything had a funny side. I was called 'Joey Brown' at home, because I was always pulling faces. We girls would laugh so much that we would wet our pants, but I was also blessed with loads of common sense and was highly practical.

While I was the most artistic of the family I couldn't do the tough stuff at school. Algebra, geometry, musical notation and shorthand — anything that involved symbols and abstract images seemed like learning Chinese to me, and I came to believe that my brain was cross-wired. I tried hard. Anything practical, I was a winner; anything academic, I just couldn't seem to get the wires to connect. I'd be sitting in an exam and I'd think, 'Goodness me, the page has gone blank!'

I just couldn't seem to get anything that I needed to say on paper. The teachers knew I wasn't stupid, and they always said I should try harder because I could do better. But I *was* trying my best and I couldn't do better. Consequently, I have no formal qualifications, but I've done well in business, so my dad was right. 'It's not your brains that count,' he used to say, 'it's your common sense.' I took him at his word, and I've used my practicality and my vision all my life.

The worst thing at school was the dental clinic, because I had terrible teeth. I have always been milk-intolerant, and that may be why I had very chalky teeth. I was told it was because I didn't clean them well enough, which wasn't true. I used to scrub my teeth until my gums bled. But I was always called up by the dental nurse, which froze the blood in my veins. I'd walk very quietly over to the 'Murder House' and sit down

The Worthington family, 1954.
Back row from left: Judith,
Patricia and Jennifer.
Front row: Dorothy, Bernard (Dad),
Nancy (Mum) and Lyndsay.

without knocking, so she wouldn't know I was there. Finally, she'd open the door and say, 'Dorothy Worthington? In here, please,' and every time I knew I was up for fillings.

There was no anaesthetic in those days, and I still shudder when I remember the sound of the drill, the vibration, the taste of blood and of the metallic amalgam chips, and the hot, dull ache in my jaw. Even the dainty cotton-wool fairies and little containers of mercury balls the dental nurse gave me to take home could not compensate for the pain and fear of the Murder House.

Throughout my school days and in the years after I went to work, my sisters and I played a lot of sport. I played representative hockey, and was the goalie for Rodney District. Dad took the whole team to the matches on the back of his rehabilitated army truck. No seatbelts in those days. He used to wear an old army greatcoat that went right to the ground, and he'd run up and down the side-lines yelling: 'Go, girls! Go! Go!' It was hilarious. I also played representative tennis and badminton — anything that called for a bat and a ball and a good eye. I loved it.

We all collected stamps. We would tear them off the envelopes, soak them off the paper, lie them out to dry then put them in our albums. We were also pretty good knittters, and made our own jerseys.

Dad had a 12-bail walk-through cowshed. From the age of 10, each of us girls started milking every day. We'd lift up the handle and push out the front of the bail to let the cow out, pull the door shut, get the next cow in and then tie her leg to the rail with a leg rope. Then we'd wash her udder with an old wet rag. This was great fun, because we could squirt the teats and try to get whoever was in the next bail with the milk, or whack them with the wet rag. Being on the receiving end of the rag was not so much fun on cold and frosty mornings.

Every morning we milked before we went to school, and

we were on a roster to milk at night as well. Each milking took about two and a half hours. Often we'd grab a piece of toast off the bench in the morning, and we'd be wiping the cow manure off the inside of our arms as we were running down the road to catch the school bus. Every now and then, Lyn or I would skive off during milking and take our time going to the toilet up at the house, so Jude would have to take up the slack. She'd get her own back by giving us a solid punch on the arm, and it took days to stop aching.

There were two types of dairy farms: those that were town milk suppliers, and the others that supplied only cream to the local dairy factory, which turned it into butter and cheese for export. We were in the second category and used an Alfa-Laval centrifugal separator to separate the cream, which was poured into a large can. Dad would trundle this down to the gate in a hand-cart and hoist it onto the cream stand for the flat-deck truck to take it to the Albertland dairy factory at Te Hana. The waste buttermilk was fed to pigs and calves, but most of it was spread on the farm, because there was no commercial use for it. If the dairy factory found fault with the cream, they would pour cochineal into the can to turn the cream pink so the farmer couldn't send it back again.

The milk tankers that took whole milk from the farms to the dairy co-ops were introduced in 1951. However, most dairy farmers didn't begin supplying the dairy factories with whole milk until a decade later. It was not until I was in my late teens, in the mid-1960s, that Dad began having his milk taken away in the tanker. First he had to build the holding tanks on a concrete deck next to the milking shed, then form a road with a wide area for the tanker to turn around.

Dad was driven to provide a secure family life for Mum and we five girls. He became one of the biggest dairy farmers in the district, and all of us have inherited this drive to excel and work hard. It's not something you're aware of; it just happens every time you go to do something. I'd never think of planting a punnet of seedlings — it's always six or seven punnets. They just love me at the nurseries.

Once Dad had begun to buy tractors, he built a huge five-bay, double-depth implement shed, the biggest in the district. He loved going to the auction sales in Auckland, and he'd come back with all sorts of bargains. For example, he bought a surplus-to-requirements army truck and loads of equipment that Mum thought was unnecessary. Neighbours would bring broken implements and machinery to him, and Dad was always making or fixing things with Jude under his feet.

Lyn and I loved playing in the sheds. There were old trucks that didn't run, so we could hop into them, swing the steering wheels and press all the pedals, making *brmm brmm* noises as we pretended we were driving off somewhere. The loads of rusty barbed-wire on the back became smugglers' treasure to us. We used to spend hours there. Mum would send us to collect the hens' eggs in the disused stables, where we kept two or three dozen hens. It was our job to forage for their eggs amongst the small hay bales, retired farm implements and chaff boxes.

Quite often we'd find a clutch that might have been there too long, and we'd take them home in a separate bucket for Mum, so she could test them for freshness before she used them in her baking. She would put them into a bucket of water, and the bad ones floated while the fresh ones sank to the bottom. When there were plenty of eggs she would rub them with petroleum jelly to preserve them over winter, then cover them with water in a kerosene tin and sit them in the bottom of the safe.

She also put the cold mutton, butter, and bacon on the leg-bone into the safe. We'd take the leg of cooked mutton out of the safe to find a fly had got in, and there would be white, wriggling maggots on the meat. Mum would search through it carefully, especially around the bone, and flick the maggots off. We kids would complain loudly, declaring we'd never

Dad trundling the cream in
a handcart to the roadside
cream stand with baby
Jennifer. In those days men
were men! Imagine how heavy
that cream can was.

Out with the old, in with the
new. Mum, Dad, Jenny and
Jude in the Rugby car taking
the horse-drawn implement
to the scrapyard.

eat that meat, but she would slice it off the bone, mince it up and serve it as shepherd's pie. We never said a word, but ate it imagining we could feel the white wrigglers in every mouthful.

If we were ever sick enough to stay home from school, we would lie on the kitchen sofa and listen with Mum to the radio soap opera, *Doctor Paul*. Mum would do some ironing so she could listen and still be busy. Aunt Daisy was always on with her 'Good Morning, good morning, good morning!' and her helpful hints and recipes. On Sunday nights we would listen to the comedy serial *Life with Dexter*, and each of us girls would take turns to stand next to the radio so we could hear better while everyone else was laughing.

Meanwhile, Mum tried to bring us up properly and give us opportunities. Most of us learnt ballet until the teacher left the district and there was no replacement. Jenny and Pat rode horses at pony club, and we were all made to learn music. Jenny played nicely. Jude thumped the keys and stormed off in a paddy. Pat played the best. I couldn't make sense of the strange letters on the paper and played by ear. Lyn wasn't all that keen and gave up.

We may not have been Youth Orchestra material, but we enjoyed mucking around in a home-grown band. Pat played piano, farm worker Trevor played piano accordion and clicked his false teeth, I played the brass candlesticks or the beer-bottle saxophone, and Lyn played the cake-tin drums. Plenty of noise and rhythm, but no class. You had to be outside to cope with the noise.

Mum also encouraged us to take part in the annual Calf Club Day. This is still a big part of life in country areas, as it's designed to help rural kids develop the skills and values they need to be good farmers. By rearing and caring for a calf from the time it is two days old until it is weaned, the kids are

Ballet lessons, Dot centre and
Lyn on the far right.

Dot and Maxine the pet calf,
ribbon and cup.

Apple Puffs

Family favourite pudding.

Serves 4

60 g butter
1 cup flour
1 tsp baking powder
1 pinch of salt
milk to mix
2 Granny Smith apples

Syrup

1 cup water
1 cup sugar
60 g butter

Preheat the oven to 170°C. Rub the butter into the flour, baking powder and salt. Mix with the milk to make a stiff pastry dough. Roll out the pastry into a flat sheet, on a lightly floured board.

Peel and quarter the apples, and remove the core. Wrap each piece of apple with pastry, and put in an ovenproof dish.

Place the syrup ingredients in the microwave on high for 30 seconds, or until the butter melts and the sugar is dissolved, or on the top of the stove and bring to the boil.

Pour the syrup over the apple puffs.

Bake for 30 minutes, basting the hot syrup over the puffs until golden brown. Serve hot with ice cream. Yummy.

encouraged to be motivated and committed, compassionate and responsible.

It's also a heck of a lot of fun and you get half a day off school. We had to groom and train our calves until they looked magnificent and performed perfectly in the ring. Their coats were so shiny you could just about do your hair in the reflection off their hides, their hooves were polished, and we had to lead them for weeks and weeks to get them used to our commands.

After all the preparation we'd go off to Calf Club and come home with a little batch of ribbons to display on our bedroom walls. One year Pat, Lyn and I had three magnificent calves. Mum was giving them linseed oil and other supplements to make their coats really shiny, but one day she must have taken the wrong jar off the shelf. She was crying as much as we were when we got up to the shed the next morning to find them dead. It was such a tragedy, because we'd spent so long looking after them and we were sure one of them would win the Champion of Champions ribbon. We had only a week to get another lot of calves ready, but we still came home with a handful of ribbons.

Mum also sent us to Sunday School. We loved the stories and colouring pictures best, but as we grew up Lyn and I would hide under the house when it was time to go to church. Mum would call and call, then finally have to go without us. We would crawl out when we heard the car drive away, then be scarce when she came home. It's not that we minded church, it was just boring sitting still on a hard seat for two hours in a little hall with a cross on the front wall. We were too young to understand any of that.

Mum did the flowers in church when it was her turn on the roster. I loved to go and help her. We always had to use what grew in the garden — there were no silk or bought flowers then.

Later, when I was travelling, I learnt to love those ancient churches of Europe with their magnificent architecture. I would sit and look in wonder at the masterpieces of skill and

Kornie Cake

I've been making this recipe for over 55 years. It's a recipe all children can easily make.

250 g (1/2 lb) butter
2 cups flour
1 cup sugar
1½ cups desiccated coconut
2 cups Weet-Bix, crumbled (or cornflakes)
4 tsp cocoa
2 tsp baking powder

Chocolate Icing

3 cups icing sugar
large knob of soft butter (approx 75g)
1 tsp vanilla essence
4 tsp good-quality cocoa

Set oven at 170°C. Melt butter, transfer to a bowl. Add all the remaining ingredients to the melted butter and mix together until well combined.

Press mixture into a buttered oblong cake tin (25 x 30cm) and bake for approximately 25 to 30 minutes or until the mixture is starting to pull away from the sides of the tin.

Mix all icing ingredients together and beat until smooth. Add additional teaspoon of water if necessary to get the right consistency. When the cake has cooled, spread with the chocolate icing then sprinkle with chopped walnuts or coconut.

craftsmanship of another era. Obviously something stayed with us, because four of the Worthington girls got married in the little wooden church in Wellsford — and one eloped.

Our mother was responsible for the family, the house and the garden. Besides feeding our family of seven, there were often three or four farm workers who also needed regular meals and laundry services.

Monday was washing day. It was strenuous work and took the best part of 10 hours. When we changed our bed linen, we had to put our top sheet onto the bottom and a fresh sheet on the top. It wasn't possible to wash both sheets for everybody. Mum had to light the copper, boil the sheets, put them through the old hand-wringer, then rinse them in cold water in one concrete tub, haul them into the second tub and rinse them again. She put a blue bag in the last rinse to make the whites brighter. She'd go down through the piles all day long, washing more delicate things together and washing the dark colours separately from the light colours, until she got to the bottom, which was the old pink woollen singlets and the men's woolly work pants. She washed these by hand.

When we came home from school, Mum was still washing and we'd have to help her hang it out. The clothesline was always over-full, and so the wet laundry would be draped over fences and hedges to get it dry. It was a huge job for the women in those days, and they still had to get morning tea, lunch and afternoon tea for the men, as well as prepare the evening meal for everyone.

It wasn't as though you could just concentrate on the washing; you had to carry on doing everything else as well. All the dry laundry went into the baby's cot in a corner of our bedroom, and we girls ironed the flat, easy things like pillowcases, tea towels, tablecloths and handkerchiefs, leaving the shirts, dresses and blouses for Mum. As busy as I am nowadays, it hardly compares to what our mothers did every day.

The farm was always under development and there was little money to spare, so the house was not the one that Mum might have dreamed of living in. We girls didn't make it any more attractive for her by knocking holes in the walls as we threw ourselves into rowdy games of blind man's bluff in the hallway. The walls were just chalkboard covered in wallpaper. Mum would come dashing into the hall and say, 'For goodness sake, girls!' She'd try to chastise us, but she could see we were having fun. But there was an enormous hole in the wall, which Dad put a piece of brown paper over, and Mum had to live with it for months until he could finally get it fixed. Or else a window would break if we hadn't put the latch on properly and the wind pulled it off its hinges. The pane of glass wouldn't be repaired for months and months, and there'd be a big piece of wood stuck over it.

Mum had all this to deal with. She didn't have nice furniture or anything decorative. Often the springs went through the fabric on the old chairs in the lounge, and if we had guests she would run around and put blankets on the seats to make them a bit more comfortable. There was no money for interior décor. She would ask and ask, but any available money was always needed for something more important on the farm.

We had a terrible old toilet about 50 m from the house. Our toilet paper was hard, shiny squares cut out of the pink *Weekly News*. You never wasted too much time out there. With five girls, Mum and Dad, and three or four men, the bucket was usually almost full. It was Dad's job to empty it. He would always say, 'For heaven's sake, girls! Go under the trees. Go down in the orchard. Don't fill up the can so much.' We hated having friends come to visit, because we were ashamed of our toilet. If you had to go late at night, you used the old joanna — the chamber pot kept under the bed alongside the big balls of dust on the linoleum floor.

I think we girls grew up loving beautiful things because we had nothing as children. Although we didn't want for love,

P.O. Box No. 602

POULTRY, FRUIT, FARM & DAIRY PRODUCE AUCTIONEERS, & GENERAL MERCHANTS

TELEPHONES: {44-480 40-619 45-731}

ESTABLISHED 1883

City Markets (ON THE CORNER)

No. 664

Auckland,　16th April, 19 32.

M r. B.L. Worthington,

WELLSFORD.

Bought of

J. JONES L.ᵈ

GENERAL AUCTIONEERS

TRADE MARK

J J
A

BANKERS:
Union Bank of Australia

TERMS—
NET CASH

Grain, Produce, Seed & Manure Merchants

HARDWARE & FENCING WIRE MERCHANTS

8% Charged on Overdue Accounts

COPY

1	side Bacon.　　37 lbs.	7½d.	1	3	2
1	25 lb. Bag R. Oats.			8	3
6	pkts. Seedless Raisins.			3	0
6	lbs. Sultanas.			3	6
2	tins Ed. Baking Pwd.			2	6
1	4oz. Bot. Van. Essence.			1	2
2	lbs. Mix. Peel.			2	2
6	lbs. Rice.			1	0
6	lbs. Tapioca.			1	2
2	Pkts. Vermicelli.			1	2
2	Pkts. Macaroni.			1	2
1	Gal. Drought Vinegar.			1	6
1	Lb. tin Gold Medal Eng. Cocoa.			2	6
12	2 Lb. tin Asstd. Jam. Oak.			15	9
6	Bots. Chow Chow.			7	0
1	7 lb. tin G Syrup.			1	8
3	Pkts. "ax Matches. Tins.			4	8
4	Lbs. Starch Sylvia.			2	8
6	lbs. Wash. Soda.				3
1	lb. Colemans Blue.			1	8
2	Lge. Tins Blk Nugget.			1	8
6	tins Sebra Stove Polish.			2	6
6	Pkts. Candles.			4	6
1	Bot. Coffee. Art.			2	7
6	Bars Wash. Soap Rec.			4	9
6	2oz. Tins S. Fern Tobacco.			9	6
2	Rolls 24 x 1 x 20 Wire Netting.	11/-	1	2	0
1	10 lb. tin Honey.			6	0
	Vinegar Jar.			7	6

£　7.　6.　7d.

Dad's shopping list, 1932.

material things were just non-existent. We wore hand-me-down clothes, made the best of everything and grew up to the old adage 'waste not and want not'. We couldn't afford a throw-away attitude, and we're all still pretty canny when it comes to getting the best out of every dollar we spend.

Mum kept a big vegetable garden with all the staples — potatoes, silverbeet, beetroot, lettuce, tomatoes, apple cucumbers, swedes, turnips, cabbages, carrots and an enormous rhubarb patch. Rhubarb with custard or crumble was a standard dessert for the men. We had an orchard with nectarines, plums and Golden Queen peaches. As a result, I have loved gardening ever since I was in primary school, where I would buy little packets of sweet pea seeds that the teachers sold as a fundraiser. I would save my pocket money and be the first in line to buy them.

Later there would be a competition, and I usually took first prize for the best vegetable garden in the class. I would go out there every night, rowing them all up very tidily and making sure there wasn't a weed. It was a big help to Mum, but I really did it to make the garden beds look beautiful, and Mum had to ask me which veges she could use.

Mum bottled and preserved everything you can think of. She loved her garden and passed that love on to all her daughters. She grew dahlias, and swapped tubers with friends and neighbours to get different varieties. Wellsford was warm enough in the winter that we didn't lift the dahlia tubers unless we wanted to divide them, so they grew in enormous clumps and made an amazing spectacle for months on end. People used to come to see Mum's dahlias, and then she would put them in the A&P show. 'Just a little entry,' she would say, and they would all be sitting up in their little milk bottles in rows, all very, very carefully chosen to make sure there were no spots or slug holes.

Even today I think dahlias are a wonderful filler in your garden, because they flower for a long time in the late summer. I buy the odd one and tuck them into the perennial

The old stable junkyard.
My favourite playground
as a child.

Label from Neil's family's
orchard, Te Hana.

borders. If you pick them and put them straight into cold water they often fade very quickly, but if you dip the ends into boiling water first they keep very well as cut flowers.

A vege hawker drove around the country roads regularly with crates of produce on board his truck. It was our delight to see so many treats, like oranges and bananas. We were usually allowed only half an orange each, as they were expensive.

Mum preserved fruit when it was in season, and she would take us to Smith's Orchards just off State Highway 1 between Wellsford and Te Hana. It had all the old varieties — Golden Delicious, Red Delicious, Lord Nelson, Cox's Orange, Giant Geniton, Ballarat cookers, Kidd's Orange, Gravenstein; then, in later years, Gentian, Splendour and Gala. It was gorgeous seeing all their ripe Dougherty apples growing around the packing shed. They were bright red and often the red tinted the white flesh. They lasted on the trees when all the other varieties had finished, and our pigs loved the windfalls.

The shed had an old wooden grader that rattled along, dropping different sizes of apples into wooden bins with sacking bottoms. The seconds — the ones that were too small or had bruises — were discarded into 20-pound cases called 'dollar rots'. Mum would buy two or three cases of those — and that's a lot of apples. We would peel them and put them into buckets of salty water, then cook and bottle them so we'd have dozens of jars of apple, which was a good staple. It was essential that the fruit was available locally, as shop-bought fruit was too expensive to preserve.

Mum had a standing order with Mr Morrison over in Warkworth for A1 Paragons and other peaches. We'd all go over to collect them, and we had to give Mr Morrison a kiss. As little girls we didn't really want to kiss this man, but we got a free peach. We would treasure it all the way home, delaying the moment when we would eat it because it was such a rare and precious treat. When we got home, Mum would put all the peaches in the lounge on newspaper, and she'd spread them out in rows to ripen in the sunlight. Lyn and I couldn't resist the peaches lined up on the newspaper in the lounge and would carefully take one each. Then we'd move all the peaches in the rows so that they looked like nobody had tampered with them.

As soon as a batch of peaches was ripe enough, Mum took them off to the kitchen and preserved them. I remember sucking the skins and stones as she was peeling them, because they were so delicious. Mum used to love entering her preserves in the local A&P show. 'It's just an entry,' she'd say, but she'd have been busy for days getting those special jars of preserves ready. She'd stack all the fruit in little rows in the jar and bake them in the oven using the water bath method. That way they never moved in the jar. I've been doing the same thing myself all my adult life.

There was always plenty of food to forage for, too. In the autumn, hundreds of mushrooms would grow in fairy rings in the paddocks and we'd pick them by the bucket full. I liked the button ones best. Blackberries grew in all the gullies and around all the creeks. The biggest, fattest, juiciest ones were on the bushes that grew around the effluent from the cowshed. There were big patches out the back of the farm, so we'd go out in blackberrying brigades and pick them by the bucketful. We always took a plank to put over the creek so we could reach the berries that grew over the water.

We blackberried for years, and they were always a staple in blackberry and apple jelly. Fruit crumbles and toppings for ice cream, too. Wild blackberries taste quite different from cultivated varieties, but they're hard to find these days. I used to have nice patches along the main highway close by our farm near Oamaru, but they are sprayed now, so I have to go down as far as Hampden to look in the forest.

Although Mum was a conscientious cook, her vegetables were limp and soggy — the way nearly every other woman cooked them at the time. And when it came to putting

What a relief when Dad bought a
machine to pick up the bales.

meat on the table, she didn't have much to work with. It was usually mutton, and we loved the scent of the roasted meat that greeted us as we came home. Sometimes Mum would buy sausages or mince, but we ate mainly mutton and Dad had to kill the sheep. We always kept a few killers, and when it was sheep-killing day Lyn and I would often creep up to the cowshed to watch. We knew a terrible thing was happening, but we had to have meat on the table. Dad would turn around and see us and say, 'Go home. This is no place for girls', but we'd sneak back and peer through the railings. Our eyes would be shut, but we'd open them up just as the deed was done. The poor sheep would be writhing on the ground, kicking. It was hard work in those days to feed such a big family.

Sometimes we'd employ foreigners on the farm. I remember a man called Maurice Beauchamp, a French Canadian. Mum couldn't fill him up no matter how much food she put in front of him, and it became a bit of a game. She'd double the size of his plate and he'd still eat it and be ready for seconds before eating two helpings of pudding.

Lyn and I played a trick on him one day. The birds used to nest in the rafters in the cowshed, and we took away the eggs and in their place slipped in a few Snifters, tiny egg-shaped candy-coated chocolates. Then we said to Maurice: 'Oh look! In New Zealand you can eat birds' eggs. They're delicious.' And we ate a few. Then we slipped the real birds eggs back in and said, 'Have one, Maurice.' So he put a couple in his mouth and the yolks poured down the side of his mouth and he was absolutely livid with us.

Summer was haymaking time, and Mum would make an enormous picnic to feed the family and the workers. The men loved Mum's picnics. Apple pie was always the favourite, but she also made bacon and egg pies, and sandwiches, and brewed tea in the thermette, a tall metal kettle heated by a fire of dry grass and twigs. Dad always had to have tea made in a teapot. After the scalding water was poured onto the tea leaves, he always turned the teapot three times, and he drank out of a fine white cup with a saucer.

Mum said she wasn't a good cook when she was first married, so she encouraged us kids to cook with her, especially as we grew older. We'd think it was romantic to cook dinner and we'd put candles on the table, and then Dad would come in and say, 'Turn the light on and blow the candles out. I had enough of those in the old days.'

One night Mum was away in town, so Pat cooked tea. She must have had the meat on too high and some fat splattered onto the element. When she opened the oven door, there was a fire that threw her against the scullery wall. Lyn and I grabbed our teddies and rushed outside, yelling, 'Help! Help! Our house is on fire!' There was no one for a mile or two who could hear us. Pat put the fire out with a bucket of water, just about the worst thing she could have done for an electric fire.

Mum came home to a shocking mess — the paintwork was black and blistered, Pat had burns to her hands and arms, and Lyn and I were not helpful, yelling and crying. Mum had to clean up as best she could, and still find something for dinner to feed everyone. As children we never understood how strong and capable she was, but I often think of Mum now and have huge admiration for her.

On Sundays we had scrambled eggs on toast, or 'Cheese Muck' on toast. The recipe came from Dad's Auntie Agnes. Everyone sat around the table before it was made, and we had to eat it immediately it came off the old coal range because it rose up like a soufflé. A cheap, easy tea for Sunday night, served with plenty of toast.

The bread for the toast came on the delivery van. We collected it on our way home from the school bus. We used to pull the loaf apart and eat what we called the 'kisser crust' — that yummy layer left behind as you pulled the two halves of the loaf apart. Mum usually only had half a loaf left by the time we walked in the door.

Cheese Muck

From Auntie Agnes, for Sunday night tea.

Serves 3

1 cup milk
4 tbsp tasty cheese, grated
1 onion, finely chopped and lightly sautéed
1 dessertspoon cornflour
2 tbsp cold water
salt and pepper
1 pinch of dry mustard
$1/3$ tsp baking soda

Put the milk, cheese and cooked onion in a saucepan and bring to the boil.

Thicken with the cornflour mixed in the cold water.

Season with salt and pepper, and dry mustard.

Stir and simmer for 5 minutes.

Just before serving, stir in the baking soda and lift immediately off the heat. Serve on toast.

We girls had job lists: set the table, clear the table, do the dishes, peel the veges, empty the rubbish, sweep the kitchen, and — worst of all — empty the joannas. There were no arguments. You just did what you were told.

I believe very strongly that parents and grandparents should teach their children to be helpful in the home. Five-year-olds can set the table and clear it at the end of the meal. It doesn't need to be a chore — it's just part of what everybody does in the house. There's no need for yelling or arguments. And I think families should eat their meals at the dining-room table and talk together without the distraction of TV and texting on cell phones.

Every night when my father came in from the farm, he changed his clothes before dinner. He made us girls wash our faces and hands and tidy our hair before we sat at the dinner table. Every night. There was no arriving, slumping down and saying, 'I don't like that.' You ate everything that was in front of you, because food was hard for Mum to get. Dad would whack you across the knuckles with the back of the bread knife if you stepped out of line.

Dad was a disciplinarian. If we did wrong, he made sure we knew about it. Before we were 12 years old, he would put us over his knee if we'd really stepped out of line, take our pants down — sunny side up — and whack us with his hand. His calloused hands were as hard as sandpaper and as big as saddle flaps. The embarrassment was worse than the whacking. It was the indignation of having your pants pulled down on Dad's knee that made you cry for a start, even before you got the whack, but the whack certainly helped. He also had the razor strop hanging from the bathroom door knob. That hurt, too, when he flicked it around our legs.

Bath night was Saturday, and we all used the same water because there wasn't enough hot water in the cylinder to fill the bath several times. On the other days we gave ourselves a thoroughly good flannelling: up so far, down so far, and so far

Dinner time.
From left: Judith, Pat, Cat,
Jennifer, Dad and wee Dot. We
took turns getting the shank.
Note the radio in the corner.

Lyn and Dot sitting on the front
tray to hold the front of the tractor
down while feeding out hay. Jude
driving, Trevor and Dad at the back.

also. On Saturday night we little ones went into the bath first, then the older ones, and Dad was always last. He would top up with hot water, get in and cover his vitals with a flannel. When Lyn and I would sneak in to clean our teeth before bed we'd snigger. He would open one eye to make sure he was covered properly. He'd fall asleep there, and wake up at 2am in freezing water with a dirty tidemark around him.

If there was a do on, Jude would bring a cream can of hot water from the cowshed to supplement the hot water that came from the hot water cylinder. The first few fights the older sisters had was over who got the first bath and the cleanest water. We usually bucketed the water out of the bath the next day to water the garden. No irrigation systems in those days. We scrubbed the bath with a mixture of baking soda and kerosene. It worked perfectly, even if it was a bit smelly.

Christmas was the most magical day of the year. Dad would find a pine tree seedling and put it in front of the fireplace in the lounge. We made all the decorations. Crêpe paper streamers hung to all corners of the room from the centre light, covering the ceiling. We made paper chains to decorate the tree, along with the box of centuries-old tinsels and baubles. We blew up balloons and hung them in bunches. All the presents were wrapped in recycled gift paper that was kept in a battered old suitcase under the bed. Everything was recycled for years. On Christmas Eve, Mum tied the presents onto the branches, and in the morning we all woke up early and raced to the tree. We were never allowed to touch anything, so we had to look carefully at all the labels to see which ones were ours.

Only after breakfast were we allowed to open our presents. The suspense nearly killed us. We were ever so helpful. After breakfast the dishes were done and the lunch vegetables prepared, then everyone gathered in the lounge. Dad was Santa.

He cut the tags that tied the presents to the tree, then called out whoever's name was on the tag. We always cut the Sellotape carefully so that the paper could be used again. We all got one good present. For me it was a doll one year, a ukulele another. It was like winning a prize. Christmas Day was the one day of the year when we had a treat of roast chicken along with the usual roast mutton. Dessert was why everyone cleared up their plates — Mum's famous huge steamed pudding full of threepences, sixpences and the odd shilling, served with custard and ice cream. On Boxing Day all of the family went to Martins Bay in the Graham Paige car for a picnic.

Every Christmas Eve, Uncle Ted and his grown-up daughter, Isobel, came to stay the night. He was Dad's brother and had a big sheep farm at Mairoa near Te Kuiti. Isobel looked after the household and worked on the farm, as her mum had died when she was a child. She told me her mother was taken into hospital in Auckland in 1942 when she was five years old and her brother, Ross, was three. Children were not allowed in hospitals, so Uncle Ted used to drive up to Auckland and parade the kids on the pavement in front of the hospital so that their mother could see them from a window three storeys up. It nearly broke my heart to hear this. Even today I can weep when I think how terrible that must have been, to be dying alone and not able to hug your own children.

Lyn and I spent six weeks on their farm during the summer holidays. We would have a little bag packed and embark on the long car trip from Wellsford to Te Kuiti. We loved it down there. So many exciting places to explore. We played in the wool shed, sliding down the sheep chutes. De-licing was done in a big concrete U-shaped sheep dip. The sheep had to swim to the other end, and it was Isobel's job to dunk their heads under with a pole.

In the paddocks were big limestone rock formations covered in native bush. We could spend all day investigating, pulling out native seedlings and replanting them into our own little gardens in the rocks. One day I pulled some pretty pansies out of Isobel's garden and took them to my garden in the rocks. Isobel was not impressed to see that her flowers had disappeared, and made me go back and bring them home again. I just wanted my rock garden to look pretty. I got a flea in my ear over that.

Lyn and I used to put holly stems into the shearers' bedclothes. They would jump into bed after a big day shearing and be pricked and scratched by the sharp leaves in the sheets. There would be yelling and cursing and threats, but we thought it was a huge joke. We would get Uncle Ted to take us to the tomo caves on the farm. We had to take torches and climb down a steep ladder to get into them. It was so exciting and scary. The caves had a running stream, glow worms, stalagmites and stalactites. It was a magic place. The sound of dripping water echoed around the caves. The neighbours had great caves on their place, too, so we would beg to be taken there as well.

Isobel was engaged to a topdressing pilot, Ernie. We liked him a lot. He taught us to swim, and would pay us a shilling if we dog-paddled up the farm creek a certain distance. Sometimes he would take us up for a topdressing flight off the airstrip at the back of the farm. We were so small we could hardly see out of the windows. Taking off was the scariest part, springing into the air with the land disappearing beneath us.

We were at the house the day Ernie's plane crashed into the hill by the airstrip and he was killed. No one knew the reason for the crash, but it was a shocking, distressing time for everyone. Even though I was very young, seeing Isobel so distraught gave us an understanding of dreadful pain and loss. Isobel later married another topdressing pilot, Gary Sefton, and Lyn and I were their bridesmaids.

Because Mum was always busy, she encouraged us to go outside and play. Lyn and I would take a wee school bag with an apple each and a biscuit or something that we could rat out of Mum's cupboard, and off we'd go. We'd be The

From left: Isobel, Dot and Lyn
at Isobel's wedding.

Famous Five or The Secret Seven going off on adventures in the bush, and we'd be gone for a whole day. I can't imagine parents today letting their children wander off to the back of a 600-acre farm for the day, not knowing where they were and what they were doing. We played in the bush and built pretend castles and secret passages; we played in the creeks and caught yabbies (freshwater crayfish). It took ages to get the courage to pick them up, because you knew they had their big pinchers out to nip you. When you did catch one and felt it wriggling in your fingers, you'd squeal and throw it back in the creek.

We used to climb trees to collect birds' eggs and nests. I still collect nests. I love the clever way they are made. You get mossy ones made by little fantails, and then big straw ones from thrushes and blackbirds. We used to take one egg down out of each nest, take it home and put a needle through it, and carefully blow out the inside before putting the shell in a little shoebox full of cotton wool. We had a competition to see how many different types of eggs we could collect, and the men on the farm would help us out. If they found a skylark, pukeko or pheasant's nest when they were getting the cows in, they'd bring us home one more egg to add to our collection.

There was always plenty of work for kids to do on the farm. Summer was haymaking time, and we girls would roll the small bales into straight lines in the paddocks to make it easier for Dad to pick them up with the tractor and long trailer. The bales were heavy and we'd be exhausted, but we had to keep going as the tractor was catching up with us. Dad expected us to get the cows in for milking on horseback on the weekends. Jenny and Pat were great with horses. They used to brush them up and plait their manes, and get into their jodhpurs and go off to pony club. Lyn had a go at riding, but she wasn't as keen as the older girls. Jude was like me — she couldn't ride to save herself.

I was the most shocking horse rider. Dad expected me to

catch the horse by offering it a piece of bread, get the bridle on, and then climb on top of a strainer post to get on its back. The trouble was I'd never been given lessons. Sometimes the horse would bolt and I'd be hanging onto its mane as it shot right up the top to the ridge, about a kilometre from the cowshed. I'd be over ditches, over drains, hanging on for grim death. When the horse finally got to the top of the ridge, it was heaving and panting, while I was exhausted from trying to hang on.

After that I could actually make it walk along, and we'd go out to the back paddock and bring the cows home. Sometimes I'd fall off and the horse would gallop home. I would have to walk behind the cows, and the horse would be home hours before me.

I left school at 16 and got a job in the Westpac Bank, enjoying every minute of the three years I spent there. At first I worked as a teller, but I also did the bookkeeping on the Burroughs — the mechanised adding machine — and typed letters for the bank manager. Once at a staff Christmas dinner he told everybody that he had given me a letter, which I'd typed very professionally except for the last sentence. Where he had written 'I would like to meet you at your earliest convenience', I had typed 'I would like to meet you at your nearest convenience'. He laughed and laughed when he read it, then retyped it himself.

After I started work at the bank, I met a young man called Neil Smith at the tennis club. He was five years older than me and very shy, but he had black curly hair and I thought he was cute. His family owned Smith's Orchard near Te Hana, where I used to go with Mum to get the fruit for preserves. We began going out together, and met at hockey in winter, at tennis club in summer and at the local dances on a Saturday night, the social highlight of the weekend.

From left: Lyn, Dot, Pat and Jude
at Pakiri Beach acting the fool.

Every little country area like Tomarata, Kaipara Flats, Matakana, Leigh, Port Albert and Hakaru had a community hall where the dances were held. Neil's father used to play piano in a band in the earlier days, and then there was the Jacques band from Kaiwaka.

On Saturday we girls ironed our best frock, with our hair in rollers, to make ourselves beautiful, and spent half the day preparing our plates. All the girls and women had to take a plate for supper, and this was a highly competitive exercise. Everyone knew who made the best sponges, cream puffs, cinnamon oysters, sponge drops and savouries. It was to your shame if there was food on your plate when you took it home at the end of the evening, as that meant that other ladies' plates were better than yours — so next week you would try harder.

In reality, taking food home from the hall reflected the huge volume of supper on offer. It was impossible, even for healthy young country people, to eat all of it. Still, next week was another challenge to come home with an empty plate.

On dance nights, the chairs in the hall were placed around the walls. The girls sat on one side, the boys the other, and we eyed each other up in anticipation. As soon as the music started, the boys would stampede to get the most popular girls, and once the first rush was over the shyer boys would take those still left sitting. All the girls wanted to be picked, and the wallflowers felt dreadful, sitting there alone while everyone else danced away. They would retreat to the Ladies to reapply their lipstick and do their hair while they waited for the music to stop, then they'd go back to the girls' side and hope they had better luck with the next dance.

The legal age for drinking alcohol was 21, and beer cost 25 shillings a dozen. Between dances the boys would sneak out to their cars at the back of the hall to drink the beer they kept in the boot, claiming they needed it for Dutch courage to ask a girl to dance. The policeman would do the rounds out there. He'd throw open a car door, reach in and produce a full bottle of beer, demanding: 'Who owns this?' Unbeknown to the youths, he had hidden it under his coat and planted it there. Then he'd grab the closest guy by the collar and demand who he was and where he was from, even though he knew exactly who everyone was, who their parents were and where they worked.

He'd confiscate the beer and assure the boy he'd be having a talk to his boss on Monday. Enough to sober any young fellow up. Once he'd gone back into the hall, there'd be a bit of shoving and swearing between the boys who wanted to know who'd left the bottle in the back of the car.

On weekends Neil and I used to go to Western Springs to watch the bike and midget car races. Neil belonged to the Wellsford Road Runners, and often on a Sunday's training he would run 48 km in his sandshoes. No wonder he needed knee-reconstruction surgery in later years. We went to the Rothman's Athletic Series at Eden Park to watch Peter Snell, Dick Quax and Murray Halberg race against the Americans. Waiwera Hot Pools was another favourite destination. During the day, family groups would take picnics to refuel after all the sliding, splashing and swimming. On Friday and Saturday nights the baths were crowded with young pashing couples. Not much swimming done then, you can bet. Everyone our age went fishing on the Kaipara Harbour or waterskiing at the Tomarata lakes, and snogging in the sand dunes at the fantastic beaches — Pakiri, Te Arai and Mangawhai Heads.

I enjoyed spending time with Neil, but I had always wanted to travel overseas to see the way other people lived and to have first-hand impressions of beautiful old buildings — especially the castles of Britain and Europe. I also knew that if I didn't go before I got married, it might never happen.

When I was 19, I met a girl called Gillian Flower at a friend's

twenty-first birthday party, and after talking for a while
we decided that, as we both wanted to travel, we should
go overseas together. The sooner the better. Within a short
time we had set a departure date. I took on a second job in
Mo Thompson's bakery in Wellsford to save more money for
the trip, and in June 1967 Gill and I were ready to leave New
Zealand. We planned to be away for about 18 months, so I said
to Neil, 'If you meet another girl who you like better than me
while I'm away, that's fine, because I can't say that I'll never go
out with anybody else while I'm travelling.'

Neil in 1967. A 'don't forget me'
memento.

CHAPTER 2

Carnaby Street Chick

Flowers and telegrams arrived from friends, everyone was laughing and hugging me, coloured streamers floated down from the deck. I felt like a film star as I waved to Neil and my family from the deck of the *Oriana* in June 1967. When we pulled away from the Auckland docks and sailed for Vancouver Island, I was ready to take on the world.

There must have been 20 girls for every guy on board. The meals were included in the price of the ticket, and there was entertainment every waking hour. By day I was playing quoits and taking part in all of the shipboard activities. By night there was dancing and music. We went ashore in Fiji and Hawaii, and threw ourselves into the Neptune ceremonies as we crossed the equator.

The six weeks of shipboard life were unlike anything I'd known before. At first, arriving at and departing each new

Passport photo, 1967.

port was a big thrill. We'd go up on deck to watch new people walking up the gangway. There'd be the usual fanfare of streamers, horns sounding, and everyone waving as we sailed off again for another port. After a while it became just another part of the day. When we got off the ship at Vancouver, Gill and I both got a terrible flu from the change of temperature, and spent the first week living in the YWCA, nursing ourselves as we worked out where to go from there, before heading to the United States.

Ninety-nine dollars for ninety-nine days! Just a dollar a day to travel anywhere in the USA on the Greyhound buses! It was a fantastic deal. We had bought our US$99 ticket through the travel agent in New Zealand and could get on the bus any time of the day or night at any place in America and get off wherever we wanted. The price of the ticket didn't include accommodation, but Gill had had an American minister in her church, Dr Trost, who organised contacts for us in several cities. If we were going to Denver, we would get a bed there and our hosts would find another connection for us, and so we travelled back and forth across the States.

Everywhere we went we were made to feel at home. Often we'd stay for two weeks at a time and return to the same families after a few more weeks' travel, so we got to know them and their neighbours well and felt we were part of the community. We were even interviewed by newspapers and radio stations in small towns. Everyone loved our Kiwi accents. The Marks, who lived on Long Island, New York, became lifelong friends, and we wrote to each other every Christmas. Then after 40 years they came out to New Zealand and stayed with Neil and me. It was wonderful to be able to return their hospitality.

Our hosts would make sure we experienced places like Disneyland, Knott's Berry Farm and the Grand Canyon. I noted in a letter home that the entry fee to Disneyland was $3 and $1.50 for a book of tickets on the rides — daylight robbery!

Still, even today there are very few Kiwis who would take tourists all the way from Oamaru to Queenstown just to give them a day out and bring them back home again.

The conversations around the dinner tables gave us an insight into some of the big issues and events of the time. It was a time of huge change in the States. The civil rights movement was at its peak. American boys from small towns throughout the country were marching off to Vietnam. One of the families we stayed with, the Wests, had very dear friends who were going off to war, and we were invited to a farewell party for them. No one knew if they'd ever see these kids again. The boys were excited at the thought of going and wanted to serve their country, but they were nervous at the same time. It was very strange and unsettling.

That year was also the height of the hippy era in San Francisco. Golden Gate Park was crowded with men and women dressed in Jesus robes with daisychains in their long hair, and the smell of marijuana was floating in the breeze. We were gobsmacked. It was like a fantasy.

The families we stayed with were amazed at our willingness to pitch in and cook dinner, clean up and generally help out around their homes. And coming from a land that lived on meat and three home-grown veges every night, *we* were amazed by what they bought at the supermarkets. Almost all the food was processed and packaged. They ate instant mashed potatoes with instant gravy. They would have packets of cake mix in their cupboards, but when I'd try to bake a cake and needed something extra to give it a bit oomph, they wouldn't have any flour or baking powder. Most people ate out, and we often went down the road to a Wendy's or one of the other fast-food outlets, where you were always given the option to up-size your meal at very little extra cost. You'd pay about $1.90 for soup, beef stroganoff and Black Forest cake with maple syrup and walnut ice cream. We tried to live on $1 a day for food, so we were grateful when people took us out for meals. My passage cost £200, and I had paid a return fare on the ship. Before we left New Zealand we sent a little bit of money to America, but we were pretty poor and we were watching how much we lived on.

We had some scary times in the bus depots late at night, because they were usually crowded with undesirables. They'd be eyeing us up as we sat huddled together nervously, with our suitcases placed as a barricade around us, and we had to use a few choice phrases to let them know we didn't want their company and had no money to give them. We had always thought of America as a rich country and weren't prepared for the number of people we saw begging for money and sleeping rough in doorways.

It wasn't just destitute people who seemed threatening. I always had in the back of my mind my father's instruction that girls should look after themselves and not give themselves away to anybody who fancied a fling, only to ditch you in the gutter the next morning. Nonetheless, we still had a few narrow escapes. One day a friend of mine from Wellsford rang to say he was surfing on the beaches around Los Angeles, and suggested we should meet at a particular bus station in the city at a particular time. Gill and I waited for hours and he didn't turn up. We decided to go back to the family we were staying with, but the guy at the ticket booth said the next bus wouldn't come for another 90 minutes and we couldn't buy a ticket until it was about to leave. So we waited for an hour and a quarter and went back to get our ticket. 'The bus has gone,' he said. We were furious. 'It can't have just left! We've been waiting here all this time and it's never been announced.'

It went on like this until there were no buses left, and he said to us, 'I'll help you. I'll take you home.' We refused at first, but then realised we were in LA, a very dangerous place at night, in this bus shelter with nowhere to go, so we said, 'OK, you can take us home.' He said he had to go back to his apartment first to change out of his work clothes.

We were really nervous when one of his friends turned up. Until then it had been two to one, and we thought we could handle ourselves. They said they would drive us home, but it became obvious that they thought they'd have a good time on the way, which wasn't part of our plan.

We were driving down the Hollywood Strip and they were trying to persuade us to try LSD, saying how great it would make us feel. At about midnight we were putting up such a fuss that they realised we weren't going to come across, so they decided to dump us in the street. We refused to get out of the car and insisted they take us to where we were staying. Looking back I'm amazed that they actually drove us an hour and a half down the road and let us out of the car. We just slammed the door and ran. That was the most frightening experience of its kind, but it wasn't the only one.

As the five months in the States came to an end, we were almost penniless. We had to pay $7 a night for a bed in the YWCA, while a hamburger cost 50 cents, and a cup of coffee 18 cents (together, the food and lodgings would cost just on US$50 in today's terms), and often we would go without eating for a couple of days. We thought of selling our blood in New York, but we looked at the line of drop-outs waiting to do that and thought we might catch something. In the week before we left the States, we rode the Greyhound buses for three days and three nights at a stretch because we had nowhere to stay and no money to pay for accommodation. When we boarded the *Queen Elizabeth* from New York to Southampton we were relieved. Now we knew we'd have decent meals for the next week. But in the five days we spent on that glamorous old tub, not once did we go to the dining room.

It was the most violent crossing you could imagine, and we were sick the whole time. It was so tremendously rough that the stewards covered the portholes so you couldn't see

New Zealand House,
our refuge in the vast city
of London.

outside. One day we asked if we could go up on deck to get some fresh air. The steward said it wasn't possible, and pulled the porthole cover back to show us the conditions. It looked as though we were in a submarine — there was no horizon. All you could see was a wall of surging, dense grey water. Even though they had stabilisers on the old girl, I'd be lying flat in my bunk and the next minute the ship would roll and I'd be looking at the ceiling of the bunk opposite. Then my stomach would be sucked flat against my back bone as we plummeted into another trough and I'd be staring cross-eyed at the floor, retching my guts out. I've never fancied the idea of an ocean cruise since then. In those days you wore cotton bras without elastic straps, so when you dry-retched the heaving motion would burst the back of your bra strap. By the time we landed in London we had no bras left, and one of our first priorities was to head for Marks and Spencer to equip ourselves.

It didn't surprise me to find that London was not in the least like Wellsford, but I couldn't help making comparisons. Wellsford was a small farming community with a main street of little wooden buildings — the butcher, the bakery, the grocer, a little movie theatre, a couple of petrol stations and more churches than you ever knew what to do with. Landing in London we were faced with this enormous city that seemed to go for hundreds of miles, and I couldn't believe how lonely you could be. You'd think that everyone would say, as they would in Wellsford or in small-town America, 'Do you need a bed for the night?' (I *was* only nineteen and very unsophisticated.) But in London nobody would speak to you. We found lodgings at the YWCA until we could get on our feet, and spent time at New Zealand House where we met other Kiwis, collected our mail and looked for flats and job opportunities on the advertisement board.

I toured London, taking in the usual sights — Hyde Park, Speakers' Corner, Marble Arch, St Paul's Cathedral, the Tower, Buckingham Palace — and was amazed and impressed with

No. 1 High Street,
Sevenoaks.

everything I saw. I learnt to love the city, and spent a lot of time down Petticoat Lane, Carnaby Street and the Portobello Market, buying mini-dresses and mini-skirts off the barrow-boys, and haggling for little glass cake plates on stands. They were five shillings each in those days, and now they are all the rage again in the shops. I would pick them up from the second-hand dealers' stands, and I had quite a collection by the time I came home. By this time I was fast running out of money and needed a job. I saw an advert in New Zealand House for a nanny in Kent, an easy train ride from London.

My employer was Mr Spiegel, an Australian dentist. His wife was a South African, and they had two young girls. The older girl, Vivienne, was at primary school, but I cared for Sharron at home throughout the day. Their house was in the wealthy private residential estate of Keston Park, near Bromley. It had been developed in 1923, covers 142 acres and is still one of the most prestigious addresses in the south of England. Each residential section is at least half an acre, and the properties are surrounded by huge areas of virgin woodland that originally belonged to the Earl of Derby's Holwood Estate. The Spiegels paid me £6 for a six-day week. A mere pittance for the amount of work and responsibility involved. They promised me trips to the continent and skiing holidays with their children, but that never eventuated.

I had never before met a woman who liked to spend the day reading in bed, or tripping off to the city for lunch with friends, while the hired help did the housework and looked after her children. The Spiegels also employed a gardener, who would always ask me for extra rations of rum in his tea when Mrs Spiegel wasn't at home. 'Just a drop more, luv,' he would say.

The family sold their house in Keston Park, so we packed up and moved to two converted oast-houses in the countryside while we waited for the grand old house in Sevenoaks to be made ready. Our new address was directly opposite the prestigious Sevenoaks School, which in turn backed onto

Knole, the magnificent estate built in the fifteenth century and once the home of Vita Sackville-West, a member of the Bloomsbury set and the creator of the fabulous gardens at Sissinghurst. The estate includes 1000 acres of parkland, and sometimes I took the Spiegel children there to feed the deer. I had Sundays off, and if Gill was busy in London I'd stay in Kent and Mrs Spiegel would lend me her little mini so I could explore the countryside.

There are 14 castles in Kent. The one that looked most like the castle of my imagining, and the one closest to where I lived, was Hever Castle, which dates back more than 700 years and was the childhood home of Anne Boleyn, the second wife of Henry VIII. It had become a ruin but was beautifully restored in the early twentieth century by William Waldorf Astor, a wealthy American. I would go from the fourteenth-century Scotney Castle at Tunbridge Wells, which has one of the best gardens in England, to Leeds Castle at Maidstone, and then around to Hever Castle and Penshurst Place, a huge rambling manor near Tonbridge.

As I made my way around this circuit, I'd drive along the most gorgeous little English country lanes, where, although I couldn't see over the hedgerows, all the bluebells and cowslips popped their little heads through the grass in spring. I would get out of the car and wander slowly, through fields of bluebells, native daffodils and primulas under the oaks and sycamores, I was fascinated by the wild plants that grew in these fields and meadows, which were soft and tame — nothing at all like our rough paddocks in New Zealand.

During the week I would take the children for walks when it wasn't raining, and I loved showing them the way the landscape changed with the seasons. In the autumn we used to kick up the leaves, and watch the squirrels running to gather the acorns and chestnuts as they came off the trees in the breeze, and rushing off with them for their little winter larders. The kids loved making up stories about the little

Hever Castle: my favourite
small castle with a moat
and drawbridge.

Hever Castle entrance, once
you're over the drawbridge.

storage cupboards inside the big oak trees, and I still collect chestnuts and walnuts for displays around my home.

At Christmas time the holly trees were covered with berries, so we'd bring big branches home and arrange them over the mantelpiece, with cuttings from fir branches and with oranges studded with cloves. The house smelt delicious. While I enjoyed my Sundays exploring Kent and going up to London to spend the day with Gill, after a while I decided that if I didn't get out of this situation I would never see anything else. My time would be up and it I would have to go home.

I decided to take a guided camping tour of Europe, but I missed my London connection with the Contiki Tour to Scandinavia and Soviet Russia, so had to travel alone by train to Belgium and catch up with the group in Brussels. As the ferry left Dover, I watched the city's huge medieval castle standing astride the stark white clifftops until it disappeared from view, and I carried the image of its towers and battlements in my mind's eye for years.

The two Contiki Tour drivers transported us in two red mini-vans. The group was made up of Australian and New Zealand girls and one boy, all aged under 25. We drove through the lowland countries into Norway, Sweden and Finland, where we were astounded at the beauty of the lakes, fiords and mountains. However, my lasting impressions of the tour came from Soviet Russia.

These days you'd probably think twice before taking a bus tour through a country in political turmoil, but most of us knew very little about Soviet Russia except that it had an extraordinary history of art and culture under the czars, while the peasants had lives of horrendous hardship. Of course, we knew it was now a communist country within the Soviet Union, but we had no idea of what to expect, because in those days there had been very few TV documentaries on

Russian soldiers surrounding a
tourist by the Tsar Bell, Moscow.
The largest bell in the world — it
has never been rung.

Dot and Judith chatting up the
guards at Stockholm Palace.
Our skirts are getting shorter!

the subject. The three weeks I spent travelling there made me appreciate the freedoms and comforts I'd known throughout my life. Things like readily available food, basic necessities in the shops, and functioning public toilets.

We were forced to sit in our mini-vans for eight hours, surrounded by guards with machine guns, when we crossed the border from Finland into Russia as we headed for St Petersburg. Being cooped up in the van for that length of time without being allowed to go to the toilet or eat was one thing, but to have men with machine guns circling the van was terrifying. Our drivers told us that it was probably part of the plan to make it uncomfortable for Westerners to visit the Soviet Union at the time. They hadn't mentioned that before we booked our tickets, although the tour operators had told us to bring extra jeans, ballpoint pens, lollies, chewing gum and anything else that we might be able to sell on the black market while we were in the country. The grim-faced guards took our passports and travel documents, and finally they got the word that we were allowed to move forward to the immigration post.

As soon as we got there, we jumped out of the van and ran straight into the building to the loos. The stench almost stopped us from going in. There was no privacy, just a set of half-height swing doors and an overflowing hole in the floor surrounded by puddles of stale urine, with thick streaks of excrement smeared on the walls. It was beyond belief. We were gagging and shrieking 'Oh God! Oh God!', but we were so desperate that there were three of us trying to go to the toilet at once. From that time on we insisted that the drivers stopped at a forest or sheltered field rather than take us to another of these so-called facilities. The parked van gave us a bit of privacy — the girls went to the left, and the boys to the right-hand side.

Meanwhile, at the immigration post the guards stripped our vans down to the seats. They pulled out all our camping equipment, sleeping bags, luggage and cooking gear. I'm not quite sure what they were looking for, but they eventually stamped our passports and we had to spend an hour or so packing everything back into the vans. When we arrived at our campsite on a farm, they took all the passports away again and we couldn't leave in the morning until they were cleared once more. That set the pattern for the rest of the trip. Aside from the waste of time, the inconvenience and the ever-present sense of physical threat, there was always the possibility that they would invent some excuse to hold our papers indefinitely or that we might be arrested on some trumped-up charge. If what we had seen so far was the civilised face of the Soviet Union, we didn't want to imagine what their prisons would be like.

We had brought books of petrol vouchers from England, and the following day we stopped at the first bowser we saw out in the countryside. A woman came out from a little shed at the side of the road. She wore a scarf around her head and a long dress down to her woolly socks with a pinny on top — the very image we had of a typical peasant. We were saying 'My God! Look at this', and falling over ourselves to take a photograph. She couldn't speak English, but her fierce frowning and emphatic shaking of her fist left us in no doubt that we weren't allowed to take photos.

The drivers gave her the voucher and she put the nozzle of a hose into the petrol tank and began to work a hand-pump. She pumped and pumped, and when the tank was full she kept pumping. The boys said 'No, no, no! No more! Full.' She shook the voucher at them and it was clear that she intended to keep pumping until the full worth of the ticket had been dispensed. The petrol poured onto the ground. We knew then that we needed to carry a couple of cans with us to take the excess. No doubt she and the other bowser operators soon learnt how to take advantage of this influx of tourists by keeping the excess to sell on the black market, but at that time they were very new to the tourism industry.

We were amazed and a bit frightened to see guards carrying machine guns standing at the corner of the side roads to make sure we didn't detour from any main road. It seemed to us that the country was still in the Dark Ages. In the rural areas, all of the houses were wooden huts, and what little paint they used was limited to a windowsill here and there. Horses and carts were used for transport and farming. Groups of women in heavy peasant clothes scythed the grass verges on the roadside, gathering every blade of fodder for the animals.

Shopping for food was a nightmare. Two of us were rostered each week to do the shopping and cooking, and, even though we had stocked up on tinned meat and other essentials before we left England, we needed to buy additional supplies. There were no advertising signs to indicate what was available, so we watched the grandmothers to see what they had in their baskets when they came out of a shop. We would go in to find the shelves almost empty. There would be three or four tins of beans on one shelf, then, three empty shelves down, there might be another few cans of something else.

You had to queue three times for every item: once to select it and get a ticket, then you'd get into another queue to pay for it, and then you'd stand in a third queue to hand over the receipt and collect the item. You had to go through this process for every single item you wanted to buy, so it took all day to get enough to feed ourselves for a week. That's why the Russian grandmothers were so important: they did all the shopping, because the mothers were out working and the children were in state crèches all day.

My father often told us that the Russian people had starved by the millions during and after World War II, but when I was younger I had never understood how that could happen. Why they didn't just go out and kill a sheep as we did, and grow their own vegetables? It was a huge awakening for me to go to a country where they had no way of providing for themselves. The seasons are not as kind there as they are in New Zealand; the winters are so harsh that literally nothing grows, and so, before they developed more modern food production and distribution systems, people lived on pickled cabbage and root vegetables.

One day we stopped to get some hot bread from a village bakery. Most of us stayed in the vans while two of the girls went inside. Within a couple of minutes we were surrounded by dozens of Russian people, laughing and smiling as they raised their kids up on their shoulders so they could look at the tourists. They were friendly and delighted to see us, and we waved and smiled at them, but were astonished to see that nearly every adult had steel teeth.

We'd never heard of such a thing, and had certainly never seen anything like it. Later we found out that it was common throughout Russia for decayed teeth to be replaced with metal caps, but when our girls came back and we tried to bite into the warm, black bread we found it so hard that we reckoned we knew why the Russians needed their reinforced dental work.

When we went into Russia we had to fill out a form listing all of the types and denominations of currency we were carrying. When we left the country, we had to produce every receipt and account for everything we'd bought. The boys and a few of the girls did a lot of trading for vodka on the black market. We could hear singing and carrying-on in the tent opposite us at night as my travelling companions used up their black-market booze.

We had only a day to visit Moscow, and, besides seeing Red Square and Lenin's tomb, we went to one of the grandest and most prestigious hotels, just to stand in the foyer and look in the luxury shops. I went to the hotel gift shop because I wanted to get a book of everyday Russian postage stamps for my collection. While I was looking at them, a group of about 12 Arabs came in wearing their flowing robes and headgear. The

Campsite in Russia. Thank
goodness for a fine night.

The Russian village where
we stopped for petrol.

one who was obviously the sheik was in a wheelchair, and the others his attendants or staff. He was wheeled to the counter and started looking at the stamps. In typical New Zealand fashion, I said, 'Oh, do you collect stamps, too?' never thinking for a moment that I shouldn't have said anything to somebody of so much importance. He didn't even look at me, but a couple of his attendants just nodded.

Our tour to the great cities of Soviet Russia left us overwhelmed at the luxury and opulence of the palaces and museums. However, when we reached West Berlin, after we'd been through the depressed places in the East, which had no neon lights and no excitement, it was as though the universe had opened up. West Berlin was all neon lights and music and beer halls. The British border guards were really friendly, and gave us a lot of cheek and invited us to a party that evening. After we'd organised our campsite, each girl dressed up in the only party frock she'd brought — for just this possibility — and we went to the dance. There were no wallflowers that night!

The blue lights that lit the dance floor made my white dress glow in the dark, and the boys told me I looked like a white angel! They put on a huge supper for us, and we danced into the wee hours; the boys being very happy to have the company of English-speaking girls for the evening. When I told one of the soldiers that we were planning to go through Checkpoint Charlie into East Berlin the following day, he explained why the Berlin Wall was there and what it meant for people on both sides.

At the end of World War II, the conquering Allied powers had divided Germany into four zones, each occupied by the United States, Great Britain, France or the Soviet Union, and the same was done with the capital city, Berlin. But the entire city had been situated within the Soviet zone, so West Berlin became a small island of democracy inside Communist East Germany. After three or four years, living conditions in West Germany had become affluent and liberal, with the help of the occupying powers, but in East Germany there were few good jobs and very little personal freedom. By the late 1950s, many people living in East Germany were packing up and heading to West Berlin. Hundreds of thousands made it across the border.

Many of those who escaped were young professionals, and by the early 1960s East Germany was losing a big part of its labour force. East Germany, with the support of the Soviet Union, tried to take over West Berlin to stop the illegal migration, and the Soviet Union even threatened the United States with the use of nuclear weapons over the issue. So, because they were determined to keep their citizens, East Germany decided to build a wall to prevent them from crossing the border.

The Berlin Wall was built overnight on 12–13 August 1961. People woke up in the morning to find that a barbed-wire fence stretched down the middle of the city, with armed guards preventing anyone from crossing to the other side. People from West Berlin who had been in East Berlin that night were trapped for decades. And East Berliners could not get back to their friends and families. The wall was rebuilt more solidly several times over the years. It was guarded by armed soldiers, and there were several checkpoints where officials and others with special permission could cross the border. The most famous of these was Checkpoint Charlie, located on the border between East and West Berlin at Friedrichstrasse.

We were amazed by the huge amount of barbed-wire and concrete traffic barriers on the roads to make them undriveable, and the vast expanse of no man's land on the Eastern side. We went through Checkpoint Charlie, which was just a little white box in the middle of the street, and were only allowed into the East for two hours. That was enough, as far as I was concerned. Nearly 25 years after World War II, the city looked as though the Allied bombing and Soviet invasion had stopped just the day before. Broken cathedrals and inner-city homes stood in heaps of rubble. People waited in long queues for food and basic necessities. There was no colour anywhere that I could see. The people wore drab clothing; there were no advertising signs anywhere. We had a drink in a pub and looked around for the two hours, feeling very disturbed, before going back to West Berlin.

I have been back to Berlin since the wall was taken down in 1989. You have to look very hard to see Checkpoint Charlie — it is surrounded by shops, and the only sign that there was of this horrendous wall is a line of bricks that follows the line where the foundations once stood. I looked at that and thought: when I was there in 1968 this was a solid concrete structure that divided two nations and separated families — one side was doing fine; the other side was in a terrible state.

I was amazed at what I had seen in the three weeks we spent in the Soviet Union and East Berlin — the poverty endured by most of the people and the fabulous grandeur of the palaces and churches in Russia's big cities. It had a huge impact, because it made me determined to take advantage of all the freedoms and opportunities we have in New Zealand compared with what so many other people have. I raised my boys to understand how lucky they were to have choices and food that half the world would envy. Even today I believe everyday people in New Zealand can afford to have a good life if we manage the money we have and don't expect to buy luxuries that put us into debt.

The tour returned to London, and five weeks later I was back on the continent with three Australian girls from the Contiki trip. We bought a little white Ford Prefect for £65; loaded the roof-rack with two pup tents, a picnic table, four chairs and boxes of food, and managed to fit four suitcases in the boot and then headed for the Dover ferry. We ran out of petrol before we reached Dover, and had to push the car to the

Fortifications in no-mans-land
in East Berlin as we travelled
through Checkpoint Charlie.

The white shed is Checkpoint
Charlie, the dividing line
between East and West.

nearest service station, where we discovered that the petrol
gauge was faulty. For the rest of the trip we kept a mileage
log so we'd know when to refill the tank. We replaced the
windshield wipers in Holland when they failed to work during
a torrential downpour, and generally coaxed the little car
through Europe.

In Holland, the image has stayed with me of the bookcase
disguising the secret stairway into the annex where Anne Frank
and her family lived while hiding from the German Gestapo
when they were rounding up the Jews. I couldn't imagine what
it must have felt like to be a 13-year-old cooped up in that small
space for so long, not able to speak much above a whisper, let
alone get out into the fresh air and run as she must have wanted
to do. She recorded the tiniest details in her journal. I can still
see their blue Delftware toilet bowl. It was beautiful to me. Her
family was rounded up by the Gestapo, and she died in a Nazi
concentration camp. I have been sad to learn that the tree that
she watched from the window as it changed with the seasons
has been stricken with Dutch elm disease.

As we were leaving Anne Frank's house, a man approached
us in the street and asked us where we were from. When we
told him, he became very excited. 'Wait here,' he said. 'Please
wait here for a few minutes.' And he took off up the street.
When he returned, he gave us a big box of chocolates. We
looked at each other, mystified. 'That's just a little token for
what your boys did for us during the war,' he said. 'I just want
to acknowledge it.' We felt so humble. My childhood had been
relatively poor by New Zealand standards, but we four girls
travelling through Europe could never begin to understand
the everyday hardships these people had suffered for so long.
That box of chocolates represented a huge price of freedom for
that man. We went on our way, very subdued.

As we drove through Germany, picnicking at vineyards
along the Rhine and sampling clusters of tightly packed, juicy
black grapes, I was thrilled at the sight of exquisite fairy-tale

castles on islands and promontories along the river. And I was in awe at the age of the buildings in the cities we visited. People were still living in four-storey houses that had been built more than 300 years ago. I would love to have gone inside to see how they lived.

We were also amazed to see the oldest profession in the world being carried out legally in the red-light districts of Amsterdam and Hamburg. The girls sat in window fronts with almost no clothes on and their legs wide open. We laughed at the procession of sailors and drunks who approached these girls, trying to bargain for their services. The prostitutes didn't like us being there and spat at us. We couldn't understand their language, but it was clear they were telling us to bugger off, even though we were no threat to their business. Not one of us wanted to swap places with them.

Everything about continental Europe came as a surprise to us. Each country was so amazingly different from the others, with languages and cultures that were nothing like their neighbours', yet we could drive from one country to the next within a day or so, and it became clear to us how easy it had been for Hitler and his army to invade these countries. As we were driving through Germany, we saw a sign leading to Dachau. Judith, one of the girls I was travelling with, said there had been a concentration camp there and, although I wasn't too keen, we decided to see it. My father had talked about how six million Jews and other minority people had died in Europe during World War II, but I didn't know the details. I thought people were taken to camps, kept on starvation rations and made to do hard manual work. I don't think I had realised that these deaths were the result of a deliberate attempt by the Nazis to exterminate all of the Jewish people in Europe, and I certainly wasn't prepared for the horrors I saw that day.

We were shown film footage the Nazis had made of people living in this dreadful place. As they arrived at the Dachau camp, the mothers and children were separated immediately, and most of the children were sent to the gas chambers. There was no chance of the parents resisting. The working-age group were sent to their barracks, and the elderly were sent to another area where they didn't survive long. They were on starvation rations with no medical care. Anyone still alive after a few months was killed anyway, because it was assumed they were somehow cheating the system.

They slept five and six people to each bunkbed, three tiers high. Cholera or typhoid were rife, but the Germans didn't try to control these diseases because that was another way of killing people off. It saved on gas and bullets. Many of the prisoners got dysentery so badly that the infected faeces leaked through the straw mattresses on the wooden bunks onto the people below.

You cannot even begin to imagine how horrendously terrible this place was. The details of the torture and excruciating so-called medical experiments inflicted on these people are more than I can bear to think about. When the Allies walked into the camps they could not believe what they were seeing. They couldn't release the prisoners immediately for fear of spreading diseases through the wider community, and they had to limit the amount of food they provided to the emaciated prisoners until their systems could cope with being fed. Once everyone had been released, the Allies burnt down the barracks. These were rebuilt later so that people could see what conditions had been like there.

The whole world needs to remember that, while a lot of the guards who worked in the camps were vicious sadists, murderers, rapists and other criminals who had been released from the prisons in the countries where the concentration camps were located, most of them were just ordinary people following orders. They may not have inflicted torture on the inmates, but they did nothing to stop what was going on. It could happen again anywhere in the world. It has happened since the war, and is still happening today in some places.

In Poland we were given another insight into what conditions were like for the Jewish people, particularly those in Poland, before they reached the death camps, when we visited a museum and saw a devastating film on the Warsaw Ghetto. Before World War II, Warsaw had a population of 1.3 million people, of whom more than 350,000 were Jewish. When Germany invaded Poland in 1939, Hitler's army rounded up the Jewish people of Warsaw and tens of thousands more from throughout Poland, forcing them to live in an enclosed compound of less than 3.5 sq km. It was surrounded by a 3-m wall topped with barbed wire. Over the next five years most of them died of starvation, exposure, and infectious diseases within the ghetto, or were deported to killing centres and forced labour camps. Many of the people in the ghetto fought back, but they didn't have the weapons to defend themselves, their families and friends.

Visiting Dachau had been an utterly traumatic experience, because the people there had no way to protect themselves from the horror and torture they endured, but learning about the Warsaw Ghetto also marked me for the rest of my life. I made the decision then to have only two children, so that if some dreadful catastrophe happened I might be able to save my two children by putting one under each arm and running. But what could I do with a third and a fourth? That was reinforced when the time came to start a family. America and the Soviet Union were still fighting the Cold War, and the whole world lived under the constant threat of a nuclear holocaust. I had no doubt that if this came about we would not be safe, even in New Zealand.

The images I saw in Dachau and Warsaw — and on another occasion 40 years later when Neil and I went to Auschwitz — have stayed with me. I always say to myself: no matter how bad times may have been for me, and no matter how much money I may have now, the only thing of true worth is the

At the gates all prisoners
passed through to enter
Dachau concentration camp.

The wooden bunk beds where
people slept three tiers high
and many to a bunk.

freedom to choose how and where I live, what I eat, where I work, and the friends I have around me. And I believe that here in New Zealand we have a system of government and a way of living that allows people to live a full and happy life. There is nothing that anyone can suffer in New Zealand that compares to what happened in Europe at that period of time.

As it happened, we were in Venice when the Russians rolled into Czechoslovakia in their tanks. We'd seen what they had to offer in their own country and didn't want any part of it. All we could think of was how to escape and get into Switzerland, a neutral country.

The trip through Italy had been exciting, one way and another. By this time our car had become a real problem. Whenever we drove up a hill the radiator boiled, steam would pour from under the bonnet, and we would have to pull over to the side of the road to let it cool down. As we were driving towards Florence, the car engine finally died and we rolled to a stop on the edge of the motorway.

I hitch-hiked with one of the girls I was travelling with to the toll-booth area, where we could ring the Italian equivalent of the AA, and then thumbed a ride back to the car. It was illegal to hitch-hike on the motorway, but we had no choice. The Italian AA had arrived by the time we got back, and they towed us to a tiny village, Pian del Voglio, that had a garage, a small hotel and an eating house. We booked into the hotel while the car went to the garage the following day.

Then we sat down in the little restaurant to eat. It was obvious that very few tourists stayed in the village, because all of the locals came along to give us the once-over, and we were a great entertainment to them as we ate the only dish on the menu. Spaghetti wasn't commonly eaten where we came from in 1968, and we had no experience in how to get that long slippery pasta into our mouths. We were in fits of laughter ourselves, and the squeals and giggles increased when we got to our rooms and were introduced to a bidet. We'd never seen

French breadsticks:
Judith and Dot on the
waterfront in Nice.

Nautical and nice
in Nice.

one of those either, and it was a far cry from the long-drop at the end of the garden path. I wasn't aware you could wash your bottom with a flush: it felt more like an enema.

The following morning we walked over to the garage, and all they could say was, 'kaputta, kaputta, kaputta'. That's what they'd said in Holland when the windshield wipers died, so we weren't accepting 'no can do' for an answer. However, we had to agree that the little Ford Prefect needed a new engine, and they managed to make us understand that it would take a week for it to be delivered and fitted. Our AA vouchers covered the cost, and we had enough left over for the mechanic to drive us to Florence, where we could stay in a camping ground until the car was ready.

After we'd packed our suitcases and camping gear into his car, he said there wasn't enough room to take all of us. The local policeman offered to drive me there, but we hadn't been on the motorway five minutes when he turned off onto a lay-by. It seemed he thought this was his lucky day.

Did I have news for him! I used the tone and language that makes farm dogs cringe, and he got the message that I wasn't just playing hard to get. We drove on in cold silence, and I was never so pleased to see my friends as when I arrived at the Florence camping grounds.

We spent five days being charmed by Florence before going back to the village to collect our car, and then we drove slowly through Italy to let the engine run in. I made a promise to myself that one day I would go back to Rome and Venice when I had the time and money to do more than trail around the tourist sites. But when I heard the news of the Soviet army storming into Czechoslovakia in their tanks, I felt a shiver go up my spine and we pushed on through the beautiful Riviera.

Five weeks after returning to London I was on board the *Orsova* heading for Auckland. The ship's fare had increased since I'd paid my £200 return in 1967, and I had to ask Dad to wire me £160 to cover the cost of getting back to New Zealand. Then I had to borrow another £60 from Gill. Of that, I had to keep £35 for the cabin steward and waiter, because that was part of the deal and the way they earned their living. I paid to have my big trunk sent ahead, packed with mini-skirts, stemmed glass bowls, Russian dolls and a Portmeirion dinner set that I'd bought piece-by-piece in London. It was the dark green 'Totem' design by Susan Williams-Ellis from Stoke, and now looks so hippyish that I never bring it out. It's still in a top cupboard at home.

London receded from view as the train pulled out of the city and I headed for Southampton, where I caught the ship for New Zealand and threw myself into seven weeks of shipboard life with not a penny to spend. The ship's photographer felt sorry for me, and I spent most of my time learning to develop the photos of balls, meals at the captain's table, and candid people shots that were displayed on a board each day. It was a very useful skill to learn, and photography is still one of my favourite hobbies.

I will always remember the trip down the Panama Canal, watching the jungle slide by so close to the huge ship. When we came to the locks, everyone was on deck to watch as a submarine rose above us on the opposite lock while our ocean liner sank below it and floated through. A fascinating piece of engineering. We docked that night outside Panama City, and I decided to go ashore. Several people tried to persuade me not to go, but I could only think that I might never have the opportunity again, so several guys said they'd come with me.

I was the only girl leaving the ship. We were ferried on lighters to the dockside, and found ourselves surrounded by sailors interested in only one thing, and with more black people than I had ever seen before. Wow, what a rough town it was in 1968! The place was crowded with bars and prostitutes. Too rough for me. We went to a tenpin bowling alley where the skittles were replaced manually, and that was adventure

Travelling companions at
the beach near Rome with a
Canadian ring-in.

Dot and friends in France.
That's our troublesome little
Ford Prefect on the right.

enough for me before we went back on board the ship.

Meanwhile there was the homecoming to look forward to. All the while I'd been away, Neil had been writing letters to me on small, pale blue aerograms. At the age of 22, he had bought a bare block of land and was trying to get a little farm together. His parents didn't have a lot of spare cash, but had gone guarantor for him. Towards the end of my travels, he was scrawling, 'Come home. Hurry up.' It was Christmas Eve 1968 when the *Orsova* docked in Auckland. I had become accustomed to seeing huge skyscrapers and cities that stretched for miles and miles. Auckland seemed so small with the little wooden houses along the waterfront.

Neil and my family were there to see this girl they'd put on the ship 18 months before, and here was this dollybird straight out of Carnaby Street. Very, very short mini-skirt. Very long legs. Lots of make-up and a very high bouffy hairdo. The photographer was watching me as I waved to Neil from the railings. Neil had dressed up in his best tweed jacket and grey flannels, and I thought he'd been caught in a time warp. There'd been no tweed where I'd been! It looked like nothing and no one had changed since I'd been away, but I knew my life could now never be the one I would have lived if I had stayed at home in 1967.

Glamour on board the PNO liner
Orsova, en route to home. A table
waiter, dining companion and Dot
wearing her only dinner dress.

Departing for our honeymoon —
Dot wearing gumboots, suit
and hat. That's Paul Shepherd,
our neighbour, leaping the fence
so he could drive us away.

The mighty Waitaki Valley —
from the Alps to the ocean.

Our garden tool rack.

A present left on my doorstep.

Cath Edmonston with lavender
in front of Riverstone Country.

The fort in the Riverstone
playground.

Bevan and Dot. Pickle
day in the Riverstone
kitchen.

© Fiona Andersen

Drummond Castle, Scotland —
something to aspire to.

Drummond Castle
formal gardens.

Mike, our eldest son, and his
family; Mike holding Jane,
Sharne, Jacob, Clayton and Aidan.

Bevan, Monique, Noa and Jordan
at the Waitaki River beach.

Neil with Ben, his best friend.

Three-year-old Jane and
her pony.

Halfway there — castle
reflected in the lake.

CHAPTER 3

Start of a New Life

After all the excitement of reuniting with my family, Neil drove me to the top of Mount Eden for strawberries and ice cream, and we started to get to know one another again.

In February, when we decided to get married, Neil went to ask Dad for my hand, and Dad gave him a lecture. 'You will get nothing from me, so you'll have to make your own way in life,' he said. 'There will be no handouts from me.' With that stern advice ringing in our ears, we drove to Auckland and bought my engagement ring from Pascoes in Karangahape Road. It was a tiny solitaire and cost $75. Then we went to Stanley Street to watch the New Zealand tennis tournament — and I kept looking at my little ring all day.

I got a job in an accountant's office working as a bookkeeper for about nine months, to pay back Gill and my father the money they had lent me. My parents had just paid for Lyn's wedding and didn't have a lot left in their coffers, so in typical Dot fashion I didn't have anything I couldn't afford. My wedding dress cost $19, and I wore an enormous tulle veil that trailed behind me to make the most of my simple dress.

We were married in the little wooden church at Wellsford, and, after a one-week honeymoon in Rotorua, we went to live on the farm Neil had bought on Wayby Valley Road, just 1.5 km from the town boundary. For the next 14 years, Neil and I milked 120 Jersey-cross and Friesian cows on 66 ha (165 acres).

Neil had worked for his father in the apple orchard after

Our wedding photo,
1969.

leaving Mount Albert Grammar School, and in 1964 he was drafted into the army, where he was given basic training as a cook. He particularly enjoyed the physical training and the good friends he made there.

The farm Neil had bought in 1965 had not been developed. It had only three water troughs, and the 12 paddocks were littered with tomo holes, which presented a danger when Neil was driving the tractor and truck. There was a stream that wandered through the middle and ended in a lovely flat bush area at the northern boundary.

Everyone said the old farmhouse needed to be demolished, but we didn't have the money to build a new one. Uncle Len, who was a friend of Neil's family, very kindly pulled down the old lean-to, because it was a fire hazard and was choked with sparrows' nests. Then he tidied the house up for us, but even so it was very basic. Every doorway in the hall had been chopped out with a chainsaw, and each one was at a different level. The ceiling beams in the lounge had been painted with creosote, which oozed out and stained the paintwork. I painted the ceiling and walls every year or two, and eventually we made a lovely home for ourselves in this ramshackle old cottage.

True to the decision I'd made while I was in Europe, we had two boys: Michael in 1970 and Bevan in 1973. We had almost no money and knew that we could look after no more than two children properly, but in the back of my mind I was also concerned about what the Cold War might bring to the world.

Like every farming family in those days, we lived very simply off the land, and for the most part grew whatever we ate. Over the years I created a show garden and hosted visitors from gardening groups. We had a large orchard, hens, and guinea pigs that multiplied so much that we had to let them out of their cages to live in the pampas hedges until one cold winter when they all perished.

Working full-time while raising two little children had its hazards. You'd never do it today, but at the time, when I went out to do the milking at 5.30am, I would leave Mike sleeping in the car outside the cowshed while Bevan slept in his bassinet in the house. One day, when I went back to the house at seven o'clock, I found him in his cot, blue and convulsing. He had swallowed his tongue. Panicking, I picked him up and ran out of the house, screaming for Neil to help me. We rushed him to the doctor and found that he had pneumonia. It gave us a dreadful fright, and from that time on I had to have both children sleeping in the car, parked outside the cowshed.

Then, when Mike was five, he got viral meningitis from the school swimming pool. We were told that it could cause any number of disabilities. I can still hear his screaming in my mind from the lumber puncture. When Mike had his strength back, for about 10 years Neil used to make him exercise and swim every day no matter the weather. There were times when I'd be in tears, pleading with Neil not to take him out, but we knew that unless we could get him through this he might never be able to do the things he wanted in later life.

Mike recovered and grew up to be smart and tough, but it took a long time to get him well. At the same time, Neil's knee cartilage collapsed while he was haymaking. I had a toddler, another child with meningitis, and a husband who was all but crippled, so I had to milk the cows, feed the calves and look after a family. Just the everyday life of a woman.

Lyn lived in Kaiwaka, 24 km north of Wellsford, so as young mothers we spent a lot of our time together just as we had as children. We'd go to Auckland once a month to get our groceries in bulk, which was the only way to eke out the budget. By shopping carefully we'd have enough left over to buy a sandwich and a cup of coffee in town for lunch, then we'd go window shopping. We could never afford to buy the beautiful new dresses, and we made all the clothes for ourselves and our families.

Welcome to my new address,
Prictor Road, Wellsford.

Wayby Valley, aerial view
of our farm.

Bevan and Mike, 1974.

Family photo taken in our
Wellsford garden, 1979.

However, one day we were looking at a window display
and I said to Lyn, 'Let's go and have a look at the new hot
pants.' The saleswoman said to me, 'You'd look astonishing in
these. You've got the perfect figure.' I stood 1.78 m (five foot
ten), had nice long legs and weighed 60 kg, so she had me in
the changing room and togged out in these hot pants before
you could say 'Jack Robinson'. They were black jersey-knit,
with braces that went over a little white jersey-knit jacket. I
couldn't get over the effect! I'd thought mini-skirts were short
when I was in England, but these hot pants were shorter.

That shop owner was a great saleswoman. Both Lyn and
I had always stuck to the rule that if you couldn't afford it,
you didn't buy it, but it took two months of visiting Auckland
to pay off our first-ever lay-bys. Instead of putting them in
our bag, we wore them up and down the street of Takapuna,
thinking we were glamorous and up-to-the-minute as we
pushed our little babies in their prams. We actually had people
saying, 'Wow! Those look spectacular on you!' We changed our
clothes in the car on the way home, though, putting the hot
pants into the shopping bag. Neil said, 'Did you have a good
day girls?' And we said, 'Yes. Lovely!'

We did that every month for quite some time to get our
money's worth, and never hinted that we had bought these
terrible hot pants. Then one day we left town early and
decided we wouldn't change until we got home. It would be
OK, we thought, there'd be no one home when we got there . . .
and walked in the door to find Neil sitting at the table having
a late lunch. The look on his face was one of utter horror. To
think that his wife had been in Auckland walking around with
those clothes on! It was absolutely amazing. We didn't wear
them after that. We felt like we'd had our hands smacked.

Neil and I milked morning and evening, and then, in the
harvest season, worked at his parents' apple orchard during
the day. We loved orchard life, and it was great fun picking
with the family, bringing our babies along, having them in the

packing shed together, and so the cousins grew up knowing each other really well. We kept a few pigs, feeding them the windfall apples, and produced delicious bacon and pork that was hugely popular at the catered fundraisers I organised while the children were growing up.

All the time we were in Wellsford we raised funds for the children's kindergarten, the school, and their sports teams. Besides the usual raffles and garage sales, we catered meals for twenty-first birthday parties and weddings, at which we served our beautiful pork and bacon. I would take the meat to the bakery, and when they'd finished baking for the day they'd put it in the big brick oven. The next day I'd take it to the Four Square store and the owner would slice it.

I learnt the skill of organising events and catering for a lot of people, and I loved decorating the hall with floral arrangements. When they were in season, I'd make baskets out of big watermelons by cutting decorative patterns on the edges and filling them with fresh fruit salad. As the kids grew out of kindy, we raised enough money to pay for a new field for the hockey club by catering weddings for up to 200 guests in the Wellsford hall.

Once, when we were doing a wedding at night, I had dressed all the girls in black skirts, white tops and little aprons, and we all looked very professional, but we had trouble getting the potatoes cooked. I usually parboiled them during the day, and then I'd finish cooking them and have them mashed just before the meal. But this night they hadn't cooked through, and Neil broke three potato-mashers before he took off running around the town trying to find another one in order to finish the job. Meanwhile I was out the front telling people that their meals would be ready soon, before returning to the bedlam in the kitchen.

My orchard and vegetable garden thrived in Northland's warm, moist conditions. I swept the tracks around the cowshed to collect the dry manure, and I'd trundle it to my garden in a wheelbarrow. We still had very little money that didn't go directly into the farm, so, in order to earn a little extra, I would get Neil to plough a little piece in one of the paddocks and I would grow thousands and thousands of onion plants from seed. When they were about 20 cm high, I would put an ad in the paper, count them out into lots of 100 seedlings, roll them in damp newspaper, and deliver them to people wanting to plant out their gardens.

I also grew sweetcorn. Neil would plant out a small part of a paddock, and when the cobs were ripe the children and I would pick the ears and take them down to the highway to sell on the roadside. I'd put up a sign where the cars could pull off, and I earned more than enough money to make it all worthwhile. Meanwhile, Neil and the two boys would hide up in the bushes, embarrassed that I was down there trying to earn some more money, but as soon as a car stopped and the people came and bought some corn they would run up to see how much money I'd made. I also made crêpe-paper flowers and sewed aprons, pot mitts and oven mitts to sell at fairs.

The boys have their own stories to tell.

Mike, whose language is pretty ripe at the best of times, has always remembered my first attempt to get him to tone it down:

> We had a lot of cousins to play with, and we often played in the orchard at our place. It had a big citrus section and a heap of apple trees down below. There were also a couple of big totara trees, and for a while we were building tree huts. There was a lot of hammering and banging, and quite often one or other of the happy little gathering would come out with some pretty colourful language. We weren't allowed to say the f-word, but

we were using it quite freely. Mum would come down to see how we were getting on and she'd hear this bad language, so she decided to put a stop to this — nip it in the bud — so she instigated a swear tin. She said, 'Righto, anyone caught swearing will have to put 50 cents into the tin.' No one wanted to be the first one to have to pay up, so we toned it down.

A while later, things were pretty quiet in the orchard, so Mum thought she'd better come along to keep an eye on these young fellas. When she arrived, one of my cousins called out, 'Auntie Dot! Auntie Dot! You've got a weta on your shoulder.'

She just grinned and said, 'Oh right, pull the other one.'

My cousin said, 'But there really is a big weta on your shoulder, Auntie Dot.'

After she'd ignored him for the third time, this big bloody weta had crawled up over her shoulder blade, and when Mum looked sideways she caught a glimpse of a couple of long feelers waving at her. She yelled, 'Shit!', and flapped at it.

And all the kids were yelling, 'Auntie Dot! Auntie Dot, you swore! You have to put money in the tin, Auntie Dot!'

Anyone who knows me will tell you that having to put money in the swear tin didn't moderate my language to any great extent.

Bevan says he learnt some of his most important lessons from Neil and me when he was growing up.

Mum was always laughing. She was the life of the room, and she still is. She was always busy: picking fruit, bottling fruit, making scones, pickling things, making us clothes. Dad was a bit quieter. We had short, sharp bursts of seeing him, because he spent most of his time out on the farm. Even though he is only five years older than Mum, he seemed to have been brought up in the old school. He always called her 'Princess', and he still does. He used to refer to sporting heroes of the 1950s and give us general-knowledge quizzes: How high is Mount Everest? Who was the thirteenth president of the USA? What was Murray Halberg's major sporting achievement? Dad was always humorous, always playing tricks on us. Why have Dad and Mum got where they are? They grew up knowing that nothing is given for free. For them, working hard was the only way to get things done. There was no easy way forward. If you want to eat a scone, make it. If you want blackberry jam, go and pick the blackberries.

All this time, Neil and I were road-running, swimming, and playing hockey, tennis, badminton and squash. We were gardening, working at the apple orchard, milking cows, rearing calves, rearing children — it was a wonderful life.

There was also a real pleasure in getting the best out of the farm. We had very fragile limestone soil, which became puggy in Northland's extremely wet winters, and the grass, instead of going into their mouths, would become a muddy porridge under the cows' hooves. So, we built a wintering barn to keep the cows off the paddocks for several months of the year. It was a rectangular, open-sided shed with two sets of cow bails on each of the longer sides, and hay-racks running in front of the bails. The fodder went in one end, and the cow manure came out the other end and landed on the concrete races. Neil disposed of the manure by backing down the race with the tractor and grader blade, collecting it below the shed in an effluent pond. The cows loved the feeding system. Neil would let them out onto a fresh pasture break for an hour. They'd eat like crazy then run back to the barn where we had fed out barley meal and hay into each stall. Cows are very smart. They learn the ropes quickly.

Wintering barns were quite innovative for those times. Mike and Bevan used to help feed the hay out into the racks in the middle of the shed when they were about five and eight, so it taught them to be part of the farming scene and develop the work ethic we had as kids, even though they didn't have to do as much as we had been expected to.

We also built a sawdust pad with sides made from old corrugated iron. We put all the springing cows there at night so we could keep a close eye on them during calving. Neil would go out with his torch to check them before bedtime, again after midnight, and again at 6am. That way he could help any cow that needed assistance calving. We never lost cows at calving time; they got nursery attention. The reason is simple and completely unsentimental: dead cows are a huge waste of money. No income from the season's milk, no cow to sell, no calf to rear and introduce into the herd with new genetics. No money.

By 1980 we had developed the farm as far as we could. Neil had improved production from 9550 kg milk fat on 50 ha, when he first bought the farm, to 22,000 kg on 67 ha the last year we were there. We had just about paid it off, but, because it was located only a mile or so from Wellsford and no one else was willing to sell their property, there wasn't the opportunity to expand. Dad wanted us to buy the home farm, but Neil wasn't comfortable with that. How would we pay the right price so that in 50 years' time there wouldn't be any argument that we'd got the farm cheap?

We felt it was far more important that we move from the district and buy a new place, leaving the family farm in its own right. Dad was very disappointed, and kept coming back to us to discuss it, because he knew he probably didn't have much longer to live. He'd had a weak heart for years, but we didn't know how sick he was at that time.

When we were kids we'd see him sitting at the kitchen table, not looking too good, and we'd say to him, 'Are you all right, Dad?' He'd say, 'I'm just having a heart attack.' When we tried to get him to see a doctor, he'd say, 'No, I've had hundreds of these.' He didn't want to go to hospital and be a burden on people, so he didn't bother. But he knew when his time had come. He sat at the kitchen table, had his cup of tea, and then said to Trevor, who was now the farm manager, 'It's time we went for a walk on Mount Misery.'

As they walked through lush grass and clover, he turned to Trevor and said, 'Who said I would never be able to grow good grass here?' And he simply fell dead where he had been standing. He was only 73. We buried him on Mount Misery. Later, when their time came to leave our world, Mum and his brother Ted joined him. We planted a pohutukawa tree with them. Our old farm has been sold and broken up now, but Dad's still up there on the mountain, where he wanted to be all his life.

Our Wellsford garden
after 13 years.

CHAPTER 4

Riverstone — 'I Like the Sound of That'

We did a lot of thinking and planning before moving from 67 ha of lush, rolling Northland clay/limestone country with a mild climate to the treeless plains, stony soil and low rainfall of the Waitaki district in the middle of the South Island. The fact that we would also be leaving behind all our family and friends made the decision all the harder.

We had looked at other options closer to home, but decided against the Waikato because land was too expensive, and against Canterbury because there was very little irrigation at the time.

The early 1980s was a good time for farming. In the South Island the cropping and sheep farmers were doing very well, but when we looked around the Waitaki area this was the only dairy farm for sale. It had been converted from sheep to dairying a couple of years beforehand, but the owners wanted to sell and there was a lot of development work still to be done. The ground was stony, there were very few trees, big clouds of dust blew down the Waitaki Valley from the Hakataramea, and there was almost no infrastructure for dairying.

However, we had to jump through a few hoops before we bought it. The BNZ wouldn't back us, even though we didn't owe any money, because dairying was very new in the Waitaki district. When the bank closed the door on us, we went to our solicitor in Wellsford, who arranged private finance at 18 per cent interest from retired people in the area who trusted us and knew our families.

When Neil first looked at the property it was 216 ha (535 acres) and had an old homestead on the lower terrace, but we weren't able to buy at that time because our farm sale in Northland fell through. Then the owners split it into two titles, thinking they'd have a better chance of selling it that way, and put a small house on the upper terrace.

We bought the top terrace block of 109 ha with a compulsory right-to-purchase clause on the rest, and bought that once the development tax law was relaxed in 1988. When we were deciding on a name for the Waitaki property, I said to Neil, 'There are three I'm thinking of. One is Stony Broke.'

He grinned, and said, 'A bit negative, isn't it, Princess?'

'What about Thistle Downs? We've got Californian thistles from here to Kurow.'

'Nope.'

And then, because our new farm was on an old riverbed and chocker with stones, I said, 'What about Riverstone?'

He said, 'I like the sound of that.'

But there was one big problem: land prices had fallen, and the amount we had spent on developing the leased land meant that the landowner now owed us money. Neil and I both had to buy suits and go to Christchurch to meet with lawyers to fight for our rights. In the end we couldn't afford to take the case to the High Court, even though we were in the right as there was one signature missing on the paperwork, so we bought the other half of the farm and paid twice for our development — the very thing we had tried to avoid.

Lyn and her husband, Grant, moved us from Wellsford to the Waitaki in their truck-and-trailer unit. It took us three days, and when we arrived we discovered that the previous owners were still living in the house, so we took our gear to the bottom shed, and then Neil and I and the children had to live in a motel in Oamaru for 10 days. It was very stressful because we arrived on 25 August 1983, just as the cows were calving, and we desperately needed to be on the farm.

And then there was the house. It was just a rectangular box sitting on a designated gravel site, with not one ounce of soil, not a tree or a shrub. It didn't have a clothesline or a footpath, and it was within 20 m of the main south road and the railway line. We just couldn't believe it. I had tears rolling down my cheeks, thinking, 'My God! I thought I'd love a new house, but . . .' Besides its location and having no soil in which to plant a garden, it had small, pokey rooms, bright orange formica in the kitchen, and lime-green formica in the bathroom. I kept saying to Neil, 'Can we move this house? Can we put it way down the paddock by the reserve where there are trees and some shelter?' But we didn't have any money to move the house, and we were so busy with calving that we couldn't do anything other than move in and just get on with it.

We started with 450 cows and a 35-bail rotary milking shed, and produced 52,000 kg of milk fat in the first season. We have now got 700 cows and are producing 287,000 kg on the original farm. The property was part of the Waitaki irrigation scheme, and we had a water allocation of 16 cusecs with access to the water for 5 days out of every 14. We quickly learnt the importance of the irrigation, because we could only grow

Moving south with our worldy
possessions, 1983.

Riverstone house when
we first arrived.

grass on the irrigated paddocks. Water meant grass growth: no water, no grass.

We use the border-dyke irrigation system, which is built into a slanting paddock. It is based on a channel at the top of the slant and a series of gates that dam the water, forcing it to flow over the edge of the channel into the paddock. Mounds of earth run the length of the paddock and prevent the water from running wild. When the strip between two mounds of earth has been covered with water, a gate opens in the channel and the water flows to the next section of mounds, preventing more water from spilling into the previously irrigated strip. A clock times the rushing water and the gates close automatically. Border dykes can let out 16 cusecs of water onto a paddock, and these days modern laser technology allows very accurate flows.

In the early days, Neil would get up in the middle of the night and drop the gates to send water to other areas of the farm to get the best out of the allocation. With paddocks covered in river stones, the water just disappeared, and it took years to build up enough humus to hold the water in the soil. Even today Neil gets up at 1am or 2am while we are irrigating to check that the technology is working as it should, because a glitch in the system can waste our water allocation and cost a lot of money with water flooding paddocks if the gate hasn't closed.

One day Neil said he would take me to catch a fish and he could guarantee I'd get one. We hadn't been off the farm for months, and I was so excited that I ran home, got out of my gumboots and overalls, and put on tidy clothes. We drove up to the cowshed and he asked me to come with him while he shifted the irrigation gates. When we got there, he said, 'There's your fish!' A salmon was swimming in a border-dyke race. It had come in with the irrigation water and was trapped. I was really pissed off that I wasn't going fishing, but Neil just laughed and said, 'I guaranteed you a fish — and here it is.' I might not have got my afternoon off the farm, but we did have a nice fish dinner that night.

For the first few years we often found salmon swimming down the paddocks, but that ceased when the fish screens were put on the irrigation outlets. Now we have to go up to the Twizel and Aoraki Mount Cook salmon farms to get beautiful fresh salmon. A lot of people fish at the Waitaki river mouth just a couple of kilometres up the road from Riverstone and catch sea salmon as they head upstream to spawn. To me, it's a long time standing on a stony bank waiting for something to bite on your line, and I'm much more certain to get fish if I ring Aoraki Mount Cook and have them delivered.

We grew to love the Waitaki Valley, with its diverse landscapes from the snowy mountains behind Kurow — the backdrop to our view from Riverstone — to the rolling hills around nearby Georgetown, and the wild, braided Waitaki River just a few minutes north of the farm. When the Milligans flour mill at Ngapara was still making flour from local wheat, I used to love taking visitors there to watch it in action just as it had been more than a hundred years before when the mill equipment had arrived from England. It's no longer open to the public, but still functions.

The fabulous limestone formations known as Elephant Rocks and Earthquakes — inland from Duntroon at the southern end of the valley — are geological masterpieces and, if you look closely, you can see fossils in the limestone. A small group of locals have set up the Vanished World fossil centre at Duntroon, which features displays of local finds, and there you can pick up a map that shows the full 90 km of the fossil trail. Not far from the fossil centre you will also find ancient Maori drawings in limestone outcrops, and further on there are moa graveyards on a farm near the river mouth. Maori used to usher the moa down there, as the river formed a barrier, allowing them to then slaughter the moa. The Willetts' Collection in the North Otago Museum in Oamaru is made up

Bevan and KC with a salmon caught
in the water race, 1985.

Irrigation water race using the
new clock device, 1985.

Starting the garden in the river
gravel. What did I ever do to
deserve this?

Planting flax outside the house
gate on the tanker track.

of Maori artefacts and moa bones that were dug up when the farm was border-dyked.

Further up the valley we have the huge hydro lakes of Aviemore, Benmore and Waitaki, where nearly everyone around here goes for summer holidays. The lakes are gorgeous in the autumn with the coloured leaves on the trees, and in the winter with snowy mountains reflections in the water. Aoraki Mount Cook, Tekapo and Twizel are just a couple of hours' drive away, so a lot of local people around here make a day of it and go snow-skiing or fishing.

Another of my favourite places to take visitors is the Parkside Limestone Quarry, where massive blocks of the famous Oamaru stone are cut out of the hillsides. It looks like a scene from the building of the pyramids in ancient Egyptian times. Close by, you'll find the beautiful paddocks of the Mitchell & Webster bird-seed operation, where acres of bright yellow sunflowers and the fat seed-heads of wheat, oats and barley wave in the summer wind.

This is an extraordinary area to farm in — not as hot as Central, because of the coastal breezes, and with only very occasional snowfalls. The rainfall is low, which is why we came here to farm irrigated land. When we first arrived, the water that was used to make power in the hydroelectric schemes was then diverted into a big holding pond and gravity-fed into irrigation canals right across the Waitaki Plains. But methods are changing. Although the gigantic centre-pivot units are very expensive to install and are unstable in the nor'westerly winds — unlike the border-dyke system, which has no moving parts — the powers-that-be have declared that they must be used as they use less water, and these huge pieces of equipment are showing up here, there and everywhere.

Oamaru is a beautiful old town, with its heritage limestone buildings mainly restored and looking grand, but now there is the problem of having them strengthened against earthquakes. It is a great service town for the farming community. The

Alliance freezing works at Pukeuri is the biggest employer, but the tourism industry, focusing on the penguin colony and the historic precinct, brings a lot of money into the area.

We have everything we need here — friendly people and an easy drive to other main centres: Dunedin, 90 minutes; Timaru, 1 hour; Christchurch and Queenstown, 3 hours north and west, respectively. Happily for me, we are also within an easy drive of Central Otago, where apricots, cherries and grapes thrive in the hot, dry climate. I love the smell of the wild thyme there, and often stop to pick some and bring it home. Now I have my own patch growing in gravel, and I use it for my savoury scones all year round.

For the first few years, we reared the calves in an old wool shed, and someone stole 10 beef calves every year until we moved them from there. That really upset me. I had put a lot of time into those calves. Besides helping Neil with the milking twice a day, I did all the bookkeeping and reared the calves on my own in the first year. I carted the milk in buckets from the cowshed in a trailer pulled by our family car, a Mazda 929, then carried the buckets up the steps into the shearing shed twice a day, and fed each calf individually. Slowly we improved our lot, and bought a vat and pump to send the milk into the calf shed. Progress!

We didn't know it at the time, but New Zealand farming was about to go through some major changes. In 1973 the Government had offered subsidies to help farmers get through the slump that hit us when the United Kingdom joined the European Economic Community and we lost our preferential trading position with Britain. By the early 1980s, some farmers were depending on the subsidies for 40 per cent of their income.

But in 1984, one year after we bought Riverstone, Roger Douglas, the Minister of Finance in the new Labour Government, cancelled all farm subsidies and deregulated the

Dressed for Heritage Week,
Oamaru, outside the museum.

The Waitaki River
rules our life.

economy. We were very lucky to have the security of our 18 per cent finance, because the bank interest rates went crazy. Also, we knew how to budget so that we always had a stable interest rate, but if you were dependent on bank finance and you were overdrawn, the interest rate was 22 per cent. And then if you were overdrawn on that, it went to 33 per cent. It's hard to imagine anyone farming under those conditions.

Rogernomics, as everyone called the new economic regime, had a profound effect on all types of farming. The combination of high interest rates and low commodity prices spelt disaster. Dairy farmers were paid monthly, which gave us a cash flow, but grain and wool farmers were paid annually, and this was an extremely difficult time for them as there was no guarantee they could pay their mortgages. The local church minister had to get a job at a pig farm to feed his family, as the local community didn't have the funds to support the small community parish.

At this time some of the established farms in the district had to restructure their farming methods. In the early 1980s I was always amazed at how many sheep were in the paddocks as we drove around the district. Now they are hard to find, and the Waitaki Valley is dedicated predominately to dairying. However, when we first arrived in 1983 there were no dairy industry service and supply centres in Oamaru. When any part of our cowshed broke down, we had to fly the parts in from the dairy supply business we'd used in Wellsford.

They put them on the plane, and we'd rush over to the Oamaru airport 3 km down the road from Riverstone to pick them up in the evening, and then Neil would spend the night fixing whatever it was that had broken so we could start milking again at five in the morning. The air service was incredibly important. The plane used to fly in at seven o'clock at night, and then fly out at seven o'clock the following morning. It was like a friend and you could set your watch by it.

My mother flew down every spring for the first few years we

were in the Waitaki. In the early years she worked in the garden with me and helped me feed the calves. As she grew older, she'd say, 'I think I'll stay inside today. I'll put the meals on and fill the tins.' She died at the age of 87 in 2001, and I still miss her. When she was about to fly back home, I'd be milking in the morning and I'd run down to the house, pick her up and get her to the airport at seven o'clock. Because it was only a hop, step and a jump to the airport, I'd leave it until the last minute. Once there was a flood on the road, and by the time we got to the terminal the plane was revving its engines. One of the passengers said, 'You would think people would come at a decent time to catch the plane.' Little did she know that I had milked the cows before I got my poor old Mum to the aeroplane. People had no concept of dairy farming in those days.

In the first season Neil and I milked the cows alone, but the following season we employed a boy for a while. His name was Brownie, and he was a really hard case. One day Neil came running from the cowshed down to where I was feeding calves in the old shearing shed, and he said, 'Dot, you'll have to take Brownie to hospital. He's shot himself. He decided to get rid of a couple of stray cats around the cowshed, and instead of shooting the cat he shot himself in the foot.' I thought, 'Oh my God! How am I going to fit any more things into my day?'

I still had dozens of calves to feed, I had to go back to the cowshed at four o'clock, and meanwhile the children would be coming home from school. I ran home, got the car and helped Brownie into the front seat. As we drove into town, all he could say was, 'Dot, I've got dreadful underpants on. I need to go home and change my underpants.'

'No bloody way are you changing your underpants,' I replied. 'You don't put decent underpants on in the morning, it's your own fault.'

We got his foot fixed up and I drove him back. And I'm sure they never inspected his underpants, but he must have been remembering the warning every mother gave her children in those days: always put on decent knickers in the morning, because you never know when you'll get knocked down by a bus (or shoot yourself in the foot) and have to go to hospital.

In the paddocks where we had no irrigation, our farmland was bare and there was no feed for the wintering. For the first several years we walked the cows away to winter grazing, and it took two days. I walked in front of the herd, knitting as I went so as not to waste time, and Neil followed behind with Tan the dog. We had to put the cows in someone's paddock overnight and continue the next day. A lot of sheep farmers were happy to graze some of our cows, because grazing a different type of stock helped to break the sheep worm cycle, and it gave the farmers another source of income. Arable farmers growing barley were also keen to graze cows over winter before they put the land back into crop again, so grazing was quite easy to find, but it was a big capital outlay.

The notorious North Otago droughts in the late 1980s forced us to find some more land close at hand. Over time we bought blocks of varying sizes from nearby properties. We slowly developed each block and, with the natural increase in cow numbers, we'd grow enough replacements and build another cowshed, and then we'd be looking for another wintering block.

The effects of Rogernomics went on until the price for milk fat threatened to go down to $2.50, before stabilising at $3.30 in the early 1990s. The interest rates went from 11 per cent to 22 per cent and as high as 31 per cent. Everyone was in terrible trouble. The poor fertility of the former sheep paddocks meant that our production was low until we made a big investment in fertiliser, which gave us a lift in production, which kept our heads above water. The typical phosphate levels in sheep pastures were 2P to 4P, whereas good dairy land requires between 24P and 40P. You need half a tonne of superphosphate per acre and lots of lime to make grass grow. Even though we were doing better than the sheep and crop farmers, it was still a difficult time and we had very little spare money.

Neil and I continued to milk the cows together, and after Brownie left we employed Sarah Jones to help us. She, like Brownie before her, lived in the house with us. When we had family come to stay, we had to put the kids on mattresses in the lounge. After a few years we built a large, airy conservatory on the east side of the house, and it has been a godsend. Besides giving us somewhere to sit and relax, the huge panes of glass invite the garden inside.

The house was still so small that we had no room for guests, so we converted our garage into a little farm-stay unit and advertised through an agency that sent us overseas visitors. It was another way to make a few extra dollars when times were tough. We had all sorts of people to stay, even though we were living very basically and developing the gardens around the house. A wealthy American couple stayed three nights. I was serving afternoon tea and they were busy telling me that they had four homes in different parts of the States so that they could enjoy all four seasons. While he was talking, the man dropped his piece of chocolate cake into his teacup and splashed tea onto my carpet and sofa. I was brassed-off as I tried to get tea stains out of the new cream around-the-corner sofa that I'd saved up forever to buy. It meant nothing to him; he barely apologised. From that day on, I thought, no matter what people have in life, they're no better than me.

On another occasion we hosted five people from Singapore for two days, and that kept me on my toes. At dinnertime on their first night I asked if they wanted to see the cows being milked the next morning. After much deliberation they said yes, and I told them that they would have to be up and dressed by 6am or they would miss seeing it happen. They were very excited as they turned in for the night. I don't think they'd ever been up that early before.

The next morning I woke them, put on a cuppa and waited. At 6.30 they arrived in the kitchen and I offered them a home-baked biscuit with their tea, and, after they had tried a piece of all the different things in the tins, we started to walk out the door. It was now 7am and I was trying to hurry them up, fitting them into pairs of gumboots and overalls while they giggled and took photos of each other. They obviously thought we milked all day, as they couldn't be hurried.

We walked the kilometre up to the cowshed at a snail's pace, and when we arrived they were in time to see the last of the cows go into the turnstile. Out in the yard a big Hereford bull was servicing a cow. Wow! They couldn't believe their eyes. Cameras flashing, much giggling and shoving. They watched the milk-tanker pump out of the silo, and the bobby calves at the calf shed sucked their fingers as we fed them. Everything was such a new experience for them.

Then they wanted a ride on the new quad bike. I let them ride behind me as we drove up and down the tanker track on Neil's new pride-and-joy. One of the girls asked me if she could drive, as she had her licence and was chauffeuring the group around New Zealand. I looked at her tiny wrists and thought there was no way she would have the strength to hold the bike on the road, but she insisted that she could do it, so I got on behind and held the handlebars with her. She kept saying 'Me try! Me try!', so I let go of the handlebars — and what happened next was literally shocking. She couldn't control the bike and we shot off the road and into the electric fence. The bike was live and the electricity was jolting through our bodies. She was screaming, and I was trying to get her clear without touching the fence. But, to be honest, I was more worried about Neil's brand-new bike.

Once we were clear, we walked back to the cowshed, leaving the bike for Neil to retrieve. It was too much excitement for one morning, and she needed to have a sit-down, but they all enjoyed their stay because it was so different from their life in Singapore. We got Christmas cards from them for a few years, thanking us for the highlight of their New Zealand holiday. We had lots of wonderful people to stay. Some were so nice we hardly liked to charge them at the end of their visit, and they left more like friends.

In the early 1980s there were so many salmon in the Waitaki River that there was an annual fishing contest. Contestants went to the Glenavy Hall about 5 km north of Riverstone, over the Waitaki Bridge, to weigh their catch. Recreational fisher folk came from all over New Zealand to take part in the competition, and some of them stayed with us. It was fun to see the prizegiving and marvel over the number of fish they'd caught. Fish numbers have declined since then and there is no longer a competition, although people still fish at the mouth and at favourite spots up the river in the season. For several years we hosted people from Dunedin and Winton who came up for an annual break. They used to book our unit for a week, and they have become good friends. We don't let out the unit any more, but use it to house the new chefs when they come to join the Riverstone Kitchen team, until they get on their feet and find a flat. I use it to store the overflow of stock from the shop, too, and it's a good spare room for guests and family.

I began to build a garden within a few months of arriving at Riverstone. At first I tried to sieve the stones and gravel from what little soil there might have been in the ground at the front of the house. I leaned an old wire-wove bed frame against the trailer and threw shovel loads of gravel onto it. I collected one barrow-load of sandy soil for every trailer-load of river stones, and so I soon realised that I would have to bring in truckloads of topsoil to put on the dry gravel bed. Getting the topsoil and cow manure involved a lot of sweat and shovelling.

Neil and I have played table tennis all our married lives. It's a good way to keep fit, and in our younger years we had competitions where I'd play for a trailer-load of cow manure and Neil played for — well, I'll leave that to your imagination . . .

We would get to the stage where I had 30 trailer-loads of cow manure due to me, and then Neil would say, 'Double or quits.' He'd be laughing his head off while he delivered a mighty serve so I'd bloody lose and then have to pay up! So one way and another, the ping-pong table has been an important part of our married life. I'm putting the table in the castle so that we can continue to keep fit, but the stakes are quite different these days.

When I was first developing the garden, there was a fashion for using dried-flower arrangements for interior décor, and so I decided to plant lavender, strawflowers, statice, larkspur — anything that I could dry — with the idea that I might be able to sell them and generate a bit of extra cash to pay for Mike and Bevan's after-school activities.

Then, because I had nowhere else to dry them, I pinned the bunches of flowers to the ceilings in every room in the house: larkspur in the hall, gypsophila in our bedroom. The boys resisted having flowers in their bedroom, so they had slender sheaves of oats and wheat, while the lounge was full of strawflowers and statice. You couldn't move for flowers. It was very beautiful.

I hadn't worked out how I was going to sell them until the Willowbridge Institute came to see the garden one day. They were having a cup of tea and one of the women asked me if the flowers were for sale. I said, 'Oh well, I'm thinking about selling them, but I don't really know how to go about it. I wouldn't have a clue what to charge.' They all said they'd buy some, and gave me what they thought they were worth, which I accepted. So they were my very first customers; I earned $70 and I couldn't believe my luck.

But the pollen from the gypsophila made my eyelids swell and I couldn't stand having it in the house much longer, so I asked Neil if he would give me one bay of his new implement shed. After much hesitation, he agreed. The flowers went into the barn and I had a sign made — *Riverstone Flowers* —

and put it out on the highway near our gate. Not expecting to attract a lot of custom at first, I opened for business on the day I went away for a garden tour of Akaroa, and one of the neighbours came in to mind the shop. It was March 1988. When I got off the bus I ran up the drive to see if anybody had been to buy flowers, and my neighbour told me that I had earned $500. I couldn't believe it! I'd never had so much pocket money before.

This was the start of a new venture for me. The dried-flower industry was huge at that time. Women came to buy my flowers, and fairly soon I needed more than I could grow, so I began buying them from other growers in the district. Then I needed to learn how to produce attractive arrangements, so I bought books and gathered ideas from American magazines.

Before long I started a party-plan business. I put together a catalogue of the designs I had to offer, and hired an agent to sell on commission. She would get women to host parties, take two or three arrangements along and display the rest in photo albums. It was so successful that I employed two women, Sharon Kingan and Isobel Mather, to help me make the flower arrangements. I put a sign on the highway that read *The Best Bloody Shop for Miles*, and the barn business bloomed, with people coming in off the highway to buy the flowers and the small lines of giftware I had begun to stock.

I stole one more bay in the implement shed each year, until I had taken over all six bays. When we ran out of space, we put in mezzanine floors. Sharon and Isobel lived in Oamaru and came out to the barn to work each day. They suggested we drop the party-plan selling and set up a shop in town to save on travel and to cater to a wider market. We found a shop towards the south end of Thames Street, Oamaru's main shopping centre, and I invited Paul McLay, who was importing Indonesian furniture and interior décor items, to share the space with me. In no time at all, Riverstone on Thames had become a very successful little business.

Meanwhile, Neil had bought a farm at Pukeuri as a run-off block to grow all the winter feed and raise our young stock. It is about 4 km northeast of Oamaru, close to the sea and only 15 minutes' drive south of Riverstone. When we first bought the property, it included an old villa, which the former owners had renovated during the wool boom several decades before. They had demolished six rooms on the east side of the house, ripped off the wrap-around veranda, changed the roof line, and replaced the original kitchen with one that would have been modern in the 1950s — ming-blue cupboards, red formica bench-top and a partition with a serving hatch.

The first time we walked through it, we saw that someone had been repairing motorbikes in one room, while horse bridles, saddles and tack filled another room, and there were holes in the ceilings and walls. It was in a very bad state.

Neil was sure we would never live in that house, and even the bank manager was all for bulldozing it, but I could see its potential. It stood on a knoll and had a 100-year-old orchard close by. The house had a 12-foot stud, and the walls in the long hall still had the original Anaglypta wallpaper. I said to Neil, 'We'll just tidy it up. We'll paint the rooms.' I chose pink for the guest bedroom, the most gorgeous Wedgewood blue for the main bedroom and lounge, and arranged for a local firm to put back the ceiling roses and cornices. My vision was to create the beautiful, elegant home I had never had; I had never given up my dream. All this time I was tearing pages from glossy magazines, gathering ideas for the architectural and décor features.

As I was driving from Riverstone to the shop in Oamaru one day, I noticed an old villa being demolished at the north end of town. I needed skirting boards for the blue room, so I made myself go in and ask if I could buy the ones they were getting rid of. They were happy for me to pay for them, and then said, 'Is there anything else you want?'

And suddenly I knew how to put the character back into

the house at Pukeuri. I arranged for a friend with a chainsaw to chop out the hallway arch because it was decorated with beautiful moulded faces and clusters of fruit. We put the front and back halves at either end of the hallway in Pukeuri and cut the doorways into arches. Then there were the tiled fireplaces, the huge front door with its beautiful leadlight panels, the moulded ceilings and the Fijian kauri kitchen, complete with a huge copper range hood and a wall oven — all the things I had never had in my life before.

I persuaded Neil to build a new veranda on the house, and put in recycled French doors leading to it from the kitchen. While all this was happening, I had bought a hoard of antique furniture that had been stored at the back of the shop I had leased in town. It had belonged to the parents of the man who owned the shop and, after I had had the pieces valued by the local antiques dealer, he was happy for me to buy them.

Everything happens for a reason in my life. Here I was with this old house that I had been trying to put together and there was this amazing old furniture you would normally never find, waiting for me in the shop I had just leased. We took it to Pukeuri, and then, as I was travelling back and forth from town over the next few months, I bought more elegant old furniture and decorative fireplaces from a second-hand shop I passed every day.

By chance I learnt that the pieces I had been buying all came from the old villa I had bought the fittings from.

The Pukeuri house was being transformed, but I hadn't finished with it yet. Meanwhile it was a lovely retreat close to the sea, where I could hear the waves pounding away on the shingle and the river stones rolling back into the tide. It was my bolt-hole, filled with the things I continued to collect over the years to use in my castle.

The girls ran the shop in Oamaru very successfully, and I went in each day to give them a hand. The business was going so well that when the Regent Florist shop in Thames Street came up for sale I decided to buy it and run it as a separate venture. I had no training as a florist, but I threw myself into it with huge enthusiasm. I would pick all my greenery from the garden and run it into town every morning, but my shop manager Leigh Steel was very cautious with what she gave me to do at the beginning. I was only allowed to put the new flowers into water and cut the stems.

Gradually I pushed my way in, saying, 'Give me a go, give me a go!' So I was allowed to do the little bunches outside the door, collect the flowers from the growers and deliver the orders. I just loved all that, and the shop did very well. When Leigh married and left to have a child, I employed Paige Gibson straight from the florist school in Tauranga and we ran the shop together.

At that time everything seemed to be gathering speed. Neil decided to buy a new farm, and we took the opportunity to move our gift shop to the middle of town, which let us diversify the stock so that we had much more furniture and giftware, and more room to display it. We were off to trade fairs and keeping up with all the trends in the magazines. However, we were often two or three years ahead of our customers. When I was stocking bright red items, they were still into pastels. I was always before my time and I still am, even now with Riverstone Country. I buy things before the local market has accepted the trend, and have to wait for the customers to catch up, and then away I go again on to the next trend.

You grow as a person as you are growing your business, and you are also growing your vision. It gets bigger and bigger, and the more you grow, the more opportunities you can see. The main rule is: never spend money you don't have in the bank. You can never buy stock that you don't have cash for, so if you have a bit of a slow time you haven't put yourself under too much stress.

Growing and picking
statice for the dry
flower barn.

We grew the Regent Florist very quickly and developed it into a great shop. It all comes down to the energy you put into a business. I gave it everything and got that back tenfold. People loved coming past and taking bunches of flowers from the front door. They weren't expensive, because we used greenery from my garden to keep the price down. One Valentine's Day we worked 36 hours non-stop. There were no more hours in the day, and people would jump the queue by walking in the door asking for flowers they could take away on the spot, which was very tricky when we still had 50 orders to do on the bench. In the end the business became a victim of its own success, and I found it more than even I could handle. I found a buyer and relinquished the shop with great disappointment, because I really enjoyed that period of my life and had learnt so much.

At about the same time, the building that housed Riverstone on Thames was sold with very little warning and we had to vacate the premises in three months. The only other vacant shop at the south end of Thames Street was a third of the size of our original shop, so I asked the owner if we could build a room with a mezzanine at the back and lease the alleyway that separated it from the next property to give us more space.

I could never just walk into a space and accept it as it was if there was the possibility of improving on it. I sealed the alley off at the road, put in a water fountain, filled huge tubs with trees and white roses, and the place looked really quite smart.

The business thrived in town, but both Sharon and Isobel were moving on to other things. Neil was powering ahead in buying and developing the farms; in 2005 our youngest son, Bevan, was talking about coming home with his wife, Monique, and I was finding it difficult to be in town every day with so much to do at home. I thought, 'Now's the time to think seriously about what I'm taking on', so I sold the shop in town, and Neil said, 'Well, you've got the barn. Just bring everything back and you can work from home again.'

Neil's implement shed, stolen
one bay at a time to turn into
the giftshop flower barn.

Progress! Riverstone giftshop
five years on.

CHAPTER 5

Riverstone Country

After the experience of running successful businesses in town, I wanted to do something exciting with the shop on the farm. It definitely needed a more imaginative look than the plain corrugated-iron siding that we'd had before we moved to town.

Neil and I had seen ghost-town attractions on our travels in the States and noticed how popular they were with the tourists, so I sorted through the photographs I had taken and came up with a design. A friend offered us a couple of derelict houses on his farm, and we chainsawed off the façades — ramshackle windows, doors and gables — and attached them to the front of the six-bay implement shed. Peeling paint on sun-blistered weatherboards gave me just the image I was looking for. The talented Maurice Ireland of Oamaru won a national award for the signwriting on the shop-fronts.

Over the years, after Bevan and Monique opened Riverstone Kitchen, we added two more shops. One had been my shade house, but it didn't look right being so close to the sparkling corrugated-iron restaurant. We pulled down the shade house and rebuilt it as a parrot aviary and fernery on the north side of the restaurant. The new building was along the lines of the early settlers' huts I'd seen in the Snowy Mountains of Australia, complete with a chimney stack, rough-sawn timber and rusty iron lining the inside of the roof. I had bought postcards of these Aussie huts and used these as a model. We call it The Shack, and it houses our country-style products — baskets, kitchenware, candlesticks, woodware and other rustic ware.

We built the second shed in the orchard behind the original shop. We got the farm digger in and lifted the mature plum and apricot trees to relocate them to the playground area. The upheaval did them no harm; in fact, the shock made them produce a bumper crop the following year. Most people would have chainsawed them down, but trees take so long to grow in this gravelly soil that I couldn't bear to do that and wanted to give them a second chance.

The shed we built in the vacated space looked like a bowling alley until I filled it with beautiful home décor merchandise — pictures, mirrors, chandeliers, lamps, thousands of silk flowers, and vases. People bring in their own vases, and we make arrangements from the silk flowers as a personalised decoration. All part of the service.

Meanwhile, once the original shop-front had been established, I furnished the street with a set of stocks, a life-sized model of a Friesian cow and calf that I bought at the Melbourne Gift Fair, a dilapidated 1929 Ford truck, and a tiny cemetery with hokey inscriptions on the tombstones — and Riverstone Country was born in 2004. Scores of people photograph it every week, and I have lost count of the men who have asked if I will let them buy the old Ford so they can restore it.

The stock in the shop is nothing like it was in the late 1980s. Besides the gift- and homewares, we now sell silk flowers, but still stock natural, dried ones and keep only enough of these to supply the local market, film-set decorators, the makers of the Tip Top bread advertisements, and the like. Hardly anyone stocks dried flowers in any quantity nowadays, so it's worthwhile continuing to dry a small quantity in the house.

If I had a dollar for every time someone asks me how on *earth* I do the stocktake in my shop, I'd be able to pay for a decent chunk of the castle I'm building.

When it comes to stocking the shop I'm actually quite disciplined, although with the amount I carry it may not look like that. I don't buy willy-nilly, and I don't buy anything unless I can pay cash for it. I follow the trends in the latest industry magazines, and use my intuition about what will sell. Women don't change their house interiors as quickly as I can change the stock, so it gradually builds up. I make a point of buying for a range of different tastes and budgets. Among the people who shop with me there's a great demand for the homely, French-country feel, but others like a more sophisticated and contemporary look.

At times, when we've been in China assessing materials for the castle, I have bought a few items for the shop. The colourful kites, Christmas lights and jewellery that I bought a year or two ago sold almost as soon as they were put on the shelves. The costume jewellery market at Yiwu was at least a kilometre long, with thousands of stands. The inexpensive decorative rings were too tempting to resist, because I knew I would have a ready market for them. There were glitzy spiders, masks, birds, butterflies and snakes, as well as the more usual large pearls, filigree and little flower styles.

I asked our interpreter, Yoyo, to help me, and as we were writing the order a Middle Eastern man came onto the stand and started breathing down my neck, which gave me the creeps. He asked, 'Do you own your own shop?' and very stupidly I said yes. After that I couldn't get rid of him. 'I love you,' he kept saying.

Hoping to offend him, I said, 'Bullshit! You don't even know me.'

'Marry me. Will you meet me later?'

Boot Hill: bookings essential.
Reproduced from a visit to
Stone Mountain, Atlanta.

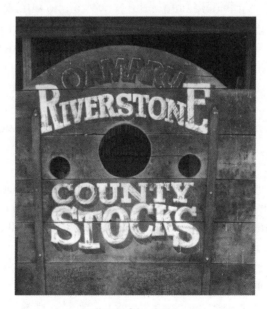

All part of the service.

'That will never happen — now, bugger off!'

Poor Yoyo and the little girl trying to write the order were becoming really anxious. This behaviour is not the Chinese way. Every time I chose a box of rings, he said, 'I will have two of those.' I had to cut my selection short to get away from this creep, who was still following me from one side of the stand to the other, declaring his love for me. We left, and I told Yoyo to go back and finish the order later. That was the first time I'd ever had that effect on anyone. Must have been the pink hair. It certainly stands out in China. Or perhaps he thought I would be a sugar momma? Well, he would have got a shock if he'd come back to New Zealand with me — no subservient woman here! When the stock arrived at the shop, the spider rings were the first to sell out.

At other times I go to the giftware trade fair in Melbourne, because it is held before the New Zealand gift fairs, and that way I get the edge on what the wholesalers will bring to Auckland. Sometimes I can pick up products that are just a bit different from anything else in the country. Because I often buy stock that won't hit the New Zealand market for another little while, it may sit on the shelves, and then someone will see it in a magazine and say, 'Oh! I've seen that at Riverstone', and people get to know where to find something they might not find in other gift and homeware shops.

Shopping at these huge gift fairs is no holiday. I come home from Melbourne exhausted. Last year the nail on my big toe split down the middle with the pressure of all the walking around the 800-odd stands at the exhibition centre and another 700 at the Melbourne Show Grounds. First, I walk quickly past all of the stands, and take two days noting the stall numbers I want to go back to. Then on the third day I consult my notes and do the serious looking for product that I think will add interest to our shop. I watch the pricing carefully, knowing I need to take into account exchange-rate differences, freight, customs duties, GST and port charges.

I try not to buy the same lines as New Zealand importers, because the much bigger volume they buy gives them better prices. On the fourth and fifth days there is a mad rush to get around all of the stands again, buying product and organising paperwork. I am so tired at night that all I can do is eat and go to bed. Then it's time to fly home and wait for the new product to arrive. Years ago I bought the big fibreglass Friesian cow that stands in front of the shop at Riverstone. I had it shipped home, and it was so big that it arrived in a courier van with its head sticking out of the window.

The Auckland gift fair is different because I deal with most of the companies on a monthly basis. Their stands are in the same positions in the halls year after year, so I know where to go. The companies do up their showrooms and present their products so beautifully, and we collect good ideas for our displays. I also know that the price shown is what I'll pay, plus freight, and it is nice to talk to the stall personnel again. They always remember me by my pink hair.

Riverstone Country is well known for our year-round Christmas shop, and we are constantly replenishing the stock. We also make to order Christmas wreaths and arrangements for the centre of tables. And because I carry a lot of stock throughout the shop, besides the constant question on how I do my stocktake, the other question everyone asks is: 'How do you dust everything?' The answer seems obvious to me: we dust the stock when we change the displays. Stock doesn't sell if you leave it in one place all the time. Anything displayed at eye level will sell more readily than something that's on a shelf near your knees, and people don't like looking above nose height. So, like all other shopkeepers, we constantly change the displays, dusting and cleaning as we go. It's a constant chore, and in the spring when clouds of pollen blow in from the farm we dust as we sell.

I have been lucky to have wonderful women to help run the business. Helen Gray has been working with me ever since we re-opened Riverstone Country in 1994, so she has grown to be my ready-reckoner. When the commercial travellers come to the shop I get Helen to sit beside me as we're doing an order, and she says, 'Got that. Got that. Got that.' I take her with me to the trade fairs and she does the same thing: 'Got that. Got that.' I say, 'Goodness! I haven't seen it. Where have you got it hidden?' I'm so busy in the garden that I don't know whether we've got it or not. Helen runs the shop five days a week, and Margaret Hastings is there four days. She has been a great friend of the family ever since we first moved to the Waitaki, and is a fantastic flower arranger, working mostly with silk flowers in the shop. Jan Harpar arrived from Christchurch after being displaced by the earthquakes, and lives in a bus at the local campsite. She works weekends with Margaret.

There are other women I can ring up and ask to give me a hand for a day when one of the staff is on holiday or when we're stocktaking, and they all just tootle along. It's a great family atmosphere. The shop has been going so long now that people who first came with their young children are now bringing those children with *their* little ones, so we have got three generations coming to see us. It's a lovely way of making a living.

The 1929 Ford truck
found under a hedge on
a friend's farm.

Interior shot of one
of our giftshops.

CHAPTER 6

Riverstone Kitchen

In 2004, just before I sold Riverstone on Thames, Bevan and Monique decided to come home from Australia. It was time for them to start a family, and they wanted to raise their children in the country, so they approached Neil and me with a proposal that they open a café on the farm.

W e were over the moon that they were coming back, but a bit surprised by their plan, because we wondered if people would come all the way out to Hilderthorpe for a cup of coffee. Besides, they had both had successful careers overseas.

Monique was a highly acclaimed musician and trained opera singer, and Bevan had worked at Terence Conran's Le Pont de la Tour and Michael Caine's Canteen in London, before moving to Australia where he became head chef at Philip Johnson's award-winning e'cco bistro in Brisbane. We were concerned that there wouldn't be enough to keep them in a quiet little backwater like Hilderthorpe, on the outskirts of Oamaru, with its population of 13,000. Still, we encouraged them.

They explained that they wanted to follow the example of

e'cco bistro and other similar restaurants in serving naturally grown local produce, and they believed they could do that on the family farm, especially as Riverstone Country had already become a destination for people travelling the lower South Island.

They moved into one of the farmhouses on the property in 2005, and helped me rear the calves that spring while they decided exactly what they wanted to build. One thing was sure: they needed to grow their own herbs and leafy greens to serve in the café. Because we couldn't grow anything in the riverbed gravel, we put in two large raised beds, filled them with straw and calf manure, and started planting out while they were drawing up plans for the new venture.

At first I thought they might set up a little café that worked in with the shop's theme and décor — maybe have people sitting around a counter on Western-style horse saddles — but they had something more sophisticated in mind. After they had come up with a few fairly modest designs, I put my hand up to say it needed to be bigger, because they were now talking about building a restaurant rather than a small café. The design they settled on was not like anything I would have chosen. A large but simple structure of shining corrugated iron with wooden power poles to support the roof, polished concrete floors and acres of stainless steel and glass. A wide west-facing deck for outdoor dining gives the customers a marvellous view over farmland to the mountains, and another faces the gardens and aviaries to the north. Everyone in the district was saying, 'Goodness me! Fancy building a restaurant in a paddock miles from anywhere.'

Neil and I had no understanding of the hospitality industry, nor did we realise how good Bevan was as a chef; we knew Monique sang beautifully and was a real go-getter, but we didn't appreciate her skills in running the front-of-house in the restaurant, so we didn't know what we were letting ourselves in for when Riverstone Kitchen opened in November 2006.

They weren't trying to make it a fine-dining restaurant. Bevan and Monique made sure everyone from family groups to farmers and truck-drivers felt welcome, but they managed it in such a way that customers enjoyed what anyone would expect of a five-star establishment — perfectly polished glasses; excellent service; and fresh, seasonal food, most of it grown in the restaurant gardens and the rest sourced from growers in the region. Actually, Bevan can tell you more about what goes on in the restaurant:

I inherited a good work ethic from both my parents, and my mother's love for feeding people. When Mum makes a meal she starts from scratch by building the soil to grow the vegetables. She did a phenomenal job of setting us up in that way, and soon after we opened everyone was talking about the quality and variety of the vegetables on our menu. People are a lot more adventurous in what they eat these days, and some of the most popular dishes included Florence fennel, cavolo nero, curly kale, fennel, broad beans, celeriac and Romanesco broccoli. In the early days, when we were deciding the day's menu specials we usually started by going outside to see what was in the garden, because the vegetables, fruit and berries were, and still are, an integral part of the dishes.

Most chefs are used to produce arriving in boxes from the markets and usually have no connection to the plants. Here, they learn how to harvest properly. There's a right way and a wrong way to harvest most vegetables, and when you're growing your own there are always a few tricks to make the most of your plants instead of simply digging them up. For example, with spring onions, if you cut them a few centimetres above ground level they grow back. And you never need to peel broad beans if they're young. Pick them early and simply eat them as they are.

I had brought in two chefs who had worked at e'cco

bistro in Brisbane to help get me started in the restaurant, but when they moved on Monique and I found it hard to attract permanent staff at Riverstone Kitchen. This wasn't Auckland or Queenstown, and there weren't many who wanted to work on a farm with no nightlife after-hours, unless you count spotlighting for rabbits and possums. One Christmas we had very few staff, so Mum became the sous chef. I was firing orders at her and she was doing her best, but putting a restaurant meal together for a table of 16, with three more tables backed up, takes more than a willingness to help out. I'd have to take a running slide across the floor, whip up the whatever-it-was I'd called for, and race back to the pans on the stoves to save the meal.

During that time Mum worked in the kitchen's baking section for months at a stretch, baking the breads and biscuits, and I can tell you it's really interesting to see a grandmother teaching a trained baker to make scones. As new chefs come to work here, she teaches them her scone-making technique. In fact, when I was working in Europe the French guys in the pastry section wouldn't share their secrets, but when I made Mum's scones one day they were so impressed they asked me if I had any more 'peasant recipes'. She was always a great baker. In the old days when ladies were asked to bring a plate, the others brought packages of chocolate biscuits whereas everything Mum did was generous. She made the biggest scones and Kiwi biscuits you can imagine.

There is an intense vibe in a restaurant kitchen, a controlled frenzy where people are working fast with fire, steam and sharp knives. Mum loves that vibrancy. She thrives on being around people with energy — people trying to achieve something — but it took her a while to realise a restaurant kitchen doesn't work the same way as the one at home. The way you talk to the others in a working kitchen is often quite abrupt, and it can seem

Bevan in the paddock where the
restaurant now stands.

The restaurant now.

© Fiona Andersen

Microgreens for the kitchen.

Just before the restaurant
opened we built these vege
plots to supply the kithcen.

Red As Her Hair Jelly

Bevan and Monique named this jelly when I first presented it to them for the Riverstone Kitchen delicatessen.

Makes 6 jars

8 large red peppers
16 small dried chillies
1 litre wine vinegar
2 packets jam-setting mix
1 cup water
8 cups sugar
red food colouring (optional)

Remove and discard the stems and seeds of the peppers, then chop them finely in a food processor and put into a large pot. Add the chillies, and rinse out the food-processor bowl with the vinegar.

Boil gently for 3–4 minutes.

Stir the jam-setting mix into the water, and add to the pot. Boil briskly, uncovered, for 5 minutes. Add the sugar and bring back to the boil, stirring frequently. Add the food colouring, if using, then boil the mixture for 4–5 minutes, until it reaches setting point. (To test that it has reached setting point, put a saucer in the fridge to cool. After 10 minutes of hard boiling, take a teaspoon of the jelly and put it onto the cold saucer. Push the outer edge of the puddle into the centre with your index finger: if it wrinkles even a little, it will set.)

Lift out and discard the chillies. Pour the mixture into sterilised jars, and seal with sterilised lids immediately.

rude, but it is just a quick way of communicating what has to be done. Mum soon learnt that there is a time to put your two cents in and other times to just get on with it. She loves working in the kitchen — any excuse to get in and order me around! But it was taking over her life. She was working with me 16 hours a day, and still had to keep the shop and gardens going. At Christmas, Monique and I gave her a present of a full chef's uniform, right down to the shoes, and she was thrilled to be formally recognised as one of the kitchen team.

Fortunately, we haven't had much trouble attracting staff since we won the *Cuisine* magazine Supreme Restaurant award in 2010 and were joint winner of the Casual Dining award in 2011, so we haven't really had to call on her services, but she sometimes complains that she is losing her touch and comes back into the kitchen for a while. She is especially useful in the sinks doing stacks of pots and dishes, and polishing the cutlery.

When she first suggested that we sell her home-made jam in the front-of-house alongside our imported deli items, I wasn't all that keen. Here we were with a slick little operation that was attracting attention within the industry, and home-made jam seemed a bit . . . mumsy. But over the years I have learnt not to tell her that something she has her heart set on won't work. When she started making her jams in the restaurant kitchen on the days we were closed, and selling them in the gift shop, she could hardly keep up with the demand. Every once in a while she would stride over to the restaurant and tell me how many more jars of jam she had sold that week. Finally she wore me down, and I said we would stock a few lines and see how they went.

Mum's now our chief jam-maker and gets into the restaurant kitchen when we are closed on a Tuesday and a Wednesday. She picks crates of fruit and berries, and she will easily make 10,000 to 20,000 jars a year. Sometimes we will put a few people around her to wash the jars and screw the lids on, and she can make a thousand jars over two days. She loves trying out recipes, and comes up with zany names like 'Picked at Night by Car Light Apricot Jam' and 'Bugger the Birds Cherry Jam' (because the birds scoffed nearly half the crop one year). There are others like 'Granny Smith's Sweet 'N Spicy Apricot, Red Capsicum and Chilli Sauce' and 'Granny Smith's Like a Night Out in Black — Raunchy and Rich Blackcurrant, Strawberry and Raspberry Jam'. It flies off the shelves, and she gets a lot of pleasure from customers' feedback.

I remember writing on the blackboard just before Bevan and Monique went to Auckland for the *Cuisine* magazine awards in 2010: *Be careful what you wish for*.

When they won the regional award and then the Supreme Award, they were as surprised as all the restaurateurs at the event who had never heard of Riverstone Kitchen. Once all the hoop-la that surrounded the event — the phone calls, texts, cards and champagne-fuelled celebrations — died down, they had to get on with running a business that had a 50 per cent increase in custom as of the night after the awards were announced. That's still the case today — the restaurant is busier than ever.

As far as I was concerned, I had to put in more effort into developing and maintaining the gardens and the grounds around the restaurant, and I needed to put in more vegetable gardens to cater for the increased demand. Neil was busy helping Mike get himself established on his own farm, so I gave my energy to helping Bevan. You do these things because they're your kids, but also because we had a lot of money invested.

After the awards were announced, hordes of families with small children were arriving for lunch and afternoon tea, so I said to Bevan, 'We really need to have something for the children to

A vege raid from the
kitchen gardens to make
chow-chow pickle.

Making apricot jam.

Dot's Chow-chow Pickle

This is a recipe given to me 30 years ago by a vet student who came to work on the farm for the Christmas holidays. She got the recipe from her grandmother.

Makes 12 jars

- 3.2 kg vegetables: green tomatoes, cucumbers, beans, cauliflower and onions
- half a litre water
- 200 g salt
- 1 kg sugar
- 2 tbsp mustard seeds
- 2 tsp pepper
- 1 litre vinegar
- 8–9 tbsp cornflour — or just enough to thicken mixture
- 2 tbsp dry mustard
- 2 tbsp turmeric

Cut the veges up, cover with water and sprinkle with salt. Soak overnight and, the next day, strain off the liquid.

Cook the veges with the sugar, mustard seeds, pepper and vinegar, saving 1 cup of vinegar to mix with the cornflour. Stir occasionally until the vegetables are soft but not mushy — about 1 hour.

Thicken with the cornflour and vinegar mixture, then add the dry mustard and turmeric.

Ladle into sterilised jars, and seal with sterilised lids immediately.

do while their parents are eating. I want to put in a playground.'
He was cautiously encouraging, saying it was a good idea but that
I shouldn't go overboard. Hah! I had already bought a collection
of books on building wooden playground equipment while Neil
and I were in the States, and I knew exactly what I wanted. Not
the brightly coloured plastic kindy-style, but something robust
and natural that would fit into the farm environment.

Here's a hint for women: never ask the family to take on a
building project for you, because you will have to go through a
big rigmarole: 'Why do you want to do that?' 'You don't really
want it, do you?' and 'No, you can't have it.' So a girl has to hire
her own builder. But first she has to save her money, and then
she can have anything she likes.

Benny Stevenson had built my beautiful henhouse, modelled
on the one Prince Charles has at Highgrove, so he and I came
up with different ideas for the structures in the playground:
swings, see-saws, a slide, a flying fox, a merry-go-round and
sturdy trolleys.

'I think we'll build a big fort,' I said to Bevan.

'Oh, don't be ridiculous,' he said. 'I don't want to look out at
a fort. It will just be an eyesore.'

'We'll make it so that it's not an eyesore,' I replied.

I designed the fort with a tower at each corner and wide
platforms about a metre off the ground. The kids can climb up
inside the towers on ladders and walk across swing-bridges.
Benny built it out of timber that has since weathered to a soft
grey. The playground takes a lot of upkeep. People don't always
appreciate that it is a private space here at Riverstone, and
they can be very rough with the equipment. They often leave it
broken for our staff to repair. You hardly notice the playground
from the restaurant anymore, because I have planted trees very
carefully to provide a screen, and it has become another reason
why so many people come to Riverstone.

I will let you in on some of my secrets, starting with jam. You need to be prepared if you are going to make a thousand jars of jam in two days. I get ready the day before I plan to make my jam. I bring the frozen fruit out of the freezer to thaw overnight, thus speeding up the cooking process as frozen fruit takes longer to cook.

If I'm making marmalade, I cut up the fruit on the first day and soak it overnight. The next day all I have to do is bring it to the boil, add sugar, boil hard to setting point, then add the magic ingredient — half a bottle of the best Grouse whisky. Neil receives a bottle every year in return for mowing a public reserve by the highway with his tractor and mower, and it is the little touch of magic I share with everyone who buys the marmalade.

My chow-chow is another popular item on the deli shelves at Riverstone Kitchen. I cut all of the veges up in 18-kg lots, sprinkle with salt, and soak them overnight in a big container. The next day I drain off the water, add all the other ingredients, and cook slowly until thickened. It's a great way of using up those caulis, zucchinis, green tomatoes and cucumbers going to waste in the garden when everything comes ready at once.

By being organised beforehand, I can rattle through hundreds of jars on preserving days, especially if Bevan gives me some extra pairs of hands to wash the huge pots and the jars before loading these into the ovens to be sterilised. At the end of an extremely busy day I get a great sense of satisfaction to see crates of product ready to restock the deli shelves.

Then there's making your own butter. It is easy compared with the way our mothers and grandmothers went about it. I was still in grandmother mode when we first moved down south. I put an ad in the paper, bought a couple of retired cream separators, and made the butter in an old hand-operated churn. It didn't take me too long to accept that the effort was hardly worth the hard work. I developed magnificent biceps, but . . . I put another ad in the paper and got an old Beatty washing machine, took it up to the cowshed and sat it up on the concrete beside the separator. Once the cream was separated, we put it into the washing machine and set the agitator to top speed.

When the butter had coagulated and the buttermilk was left slopping around in the bowl, I turned the machine off, pulled the bung out and emptied the buttermilk into a bucket. The butter then had to be washed, so I put the bung back, inserted the cold-water hose from the shed, and washed and drained the butter two or three times to clear all the buttermilk out of it. Then — and I had to use a bit of muscle here to get the water out of the butter — I put it in butter pats and slapped it on the bench. We made 50 lb or 60 lb in a session, stored it in the freezer, and it kept us going for a long time.

I have tried to make big quantities in the kitchen whizz, but I wouldn't recommend that — it ends up burning out your whizz. However, if you want to make a small amount for a dinner party, just pop your cream in the kitchen whizz and it will quickly turn into butter. Wash it thoroughly to get the buttermilk out, otherwise when you cut it globules of water pop out and it doesn't keep very long. Then pat it with a clean tea towel and sprinkle it with Maldon salt, roll it up and cut it into little cubes. You can also roll it with a butter roller or baller, so that you can use it on the dinner-party table.

In the days when I was making big quantities of butter at the cowshed, a group of students came for work experience. I was exhausting myself turning the handle of the butter churn when one smartarse was giving me cheek, suggesting he could do it so much faster. 'Great,' I thought, 'a lesson about to be learnt here', so I said, 'OK — your turn.'

He stepped forward and started putting all his energy into churning the cream, but I hadn't told him that he had to put the lid on tightly. The next moment the lid came flying off and he was covered in cream from head to foot. I had to leave the room for a moment to compose myself, and then came back to hose him down. Funnily, he never offered to help again, and nor did he make any smart comments to me. I still smile when I see it in my mind's eye.

One of my favourite pastimes is foraging for the wild apples, crab apples, plums, blackberries, elderberries and even rowanberries that grow on the side of farm tracks, back roads and highways. I have discovered certain trees that have grown from the cores and stones thrown out of car windows. The apples and plums often revert to their root stock, and I have even got a secret Golden Delicious apple tree. I was so delighted to find it, because you can't find those apples in the shops anymore and the fruit on this tree are enormous! They would be as big as a good-sized mango, and they don't have a mark on them. It is almost unbelievable. When I grow fruit in my garden they get covered in brown spots, and you have to be careful how you water so that you don't blemish the fruit. But these wild ones grow in gravel with no care or attention.

Wild apples have a lot of pectin and make your jelly set really well. I have my favourite trees in secret locations around the district, and I know when they are ready for harvesting. They have different uses in the jam-making process; some are great for preserving as diced fruit because they don't break up, and others smash up and just melt into jellies so they make really good pectin to set the jams.

Another of my favourite activities is to go to the orchards to pick my own fruit. I travel down to Central to get apricots, cherries and boysenberries in Cromwell. In the season I spend a lot of time at Barry Little's berry farm at Willowbridge, a few kilometres north of Riverstone. Barry grows the most amazing black raspberries, tons of red raspberries, and a boysenberry–blackberry cross called a karakaberry. People confuse the name with the poisonous berries of the native karaka tree, but these are a large, luscious berry, nearly 4 cm long, and they just drip off the vines so they are easy to pick.

Barry lets me pick my own because I do it in commercial quantities for the restaurant. In the season I pick them all day, and come home with the back of my ute full of buckets of berries. I freeze them straight away in 2 kg bags, so they are handy for making jam for the rest of the season.

Leanne Mattsinger looks like a little fashion model even when she is tearing around on a tractor tending her strawberry farm at the end of Seven Mile Road here in North Otago. She wears gorgeous clothes, beautiful sun hats and sunglasses, and she is absolutely thriving on producing the most wonderful berries, which she sells to the public from a stall in the garage at her house. This woman is yet another of the remarkable North Otago people who are doing extraordinary things. I get a lot of my prime berries from her and have never found better anywhere else, but I will also buy her seconds for making jam.

As I write this, the gooseberries are about to ripen and the bushes in my garden are laden with them. I leave the weeds to grow around the bushes to keep the birds off them. The berries grow on the most thorny bushes imaginable, and you need to wear thick gloves, long pants and gumboots when you are harvesting them. I make gooseberry and elderflower jam, gooseberry and strawberry jam, gooseberry pies, and gooseberry chutney. We top-and-tail the crop, and freeze the berries so they are ready to use.

I like to mix different types of berries together to produce very rich vitamin C and antioxidant blends; for example, blackcurrant, Black Doris plums, black raspberries and boysenberries. You mix the whole lot together, and it gives you this absolutely unbelievable jam. One of our most popular jams is rhubarb and ginger. As soon as the rhubarb comes into season, we pick most of it for making jam, and it is incredibly popular with the customers. The last batch sold out in two weeks, because you can't buy these old-fashioned jams on the shelf in the supermarket.

Bevan got in first with the story about how he didn't want to

A taste like no other —
homemade butter.

The plate seat outside the hen
run. It's made from the broken
plates from Riverstone Kitchen.

stock my jam in the restaurant and then changed his mind . . . I'm not one to say 'I told you so', but I can't help but be chuffed with the success of the jam-making venture for the restaurant. For Christmas last year, the girls made gift boxes — three jars of different jams to a box — and customers were buying them as presents for staff, family and friends. One person bought 50-odd boxes of the preserves as staff presents.

Most people read novels; I read jam books. I have lost count of the number of these books I have got on my shelves, because I always find new techniques, hints and tips, and I find the folklore that relates to jams and jellies fascinating. You learn intriguing pieces of information, like the fact that people used to hang rowan berries in their houses to ward off witches and evil spells.

On holiday in South Africa we visited a little town called Knysna on the Garden Route, and while everybody was having lunch I went into a bookshop where I found a jam-making book published in England. Every recipe is a gem, and with the volume of product I have made from that book I would have paid for it a hundred thousand times over. Literally! I found another book in England by a man who as a young boy used to make jam with his grandmother and later developed a method using no sugar. Instead, he uses boiled-down grape juice to set and sweeten it, and now has a successful business using this method. It is a relatively complex and costly method, but I am very keen to try it if I can get an affordable source of the raw grape juice.

I also collect recipe books on my travels, and I love reading the old-time ingredient lists. I have some from the Smoky Mountains — first you have to trap the animal to get the meat! I also have some slave recipe books from the USA's deep South. They are like reading a lesson in history, and I'm always surprised at how they managed to produce such good meals when they were cooking over open fires. How to make moonshine intrigued me, too.

Like a Night Out in Black

The elegance and sophistication of the rich black fruits and berries in this jam remind me of the days when every girl had a Little Black Dress for special occasions. That is why I call it 'Like a Night Out in Black'.

Makes 8 jars

500 g each: blueberries, cherries, blackcurrants, black
   raspberries and strawberries
2.5 kg sugar
juice of 1 lemon (strain the pips)
small knob of butter

Slice the strawberries into small pieces.

Cook all of the fruit and berries together, stirring continually until the juices have been released.

Add the sugar, and stir until dissolved. Add the lemon juice.

Boil to setting point. (To see how to test for the setting point, see the Red As Her Hair Jelly recipe on page 158.) Add the butter to dissolve the scum.

Ladle into sterilised jars, and seal with sterilised lids immediately.

Dot's Plain Scones

This recipe was passed down to me from Nana, my mother's mother, and I have passed it on to both my sons and to all the chefs at Riverstone Kitchen.

Hints and techniques

- Always make sure that you don't over-moisturise the dough. Don't add all of the milk at once, because on cold days the ingredients blend differently from how they do on a hot day. Add two-thirds of the milk, stir it in with a dinner knife to keep the air in the mix and then add as much of the rest of the milk as necessary until it is a firm dough, not a soft, floppy dough. If you add too much liquid, the scones won't rise and hold.

- The quicker you make them the better they are, so if you are adding ingredients to the plain scone mixture have them chopped and ready to go before you start making the dough.

- Make sure the oven has been brought up to the right temperature of 170°C well before you put the scones in.

- Whip the bread knife around the ingredients until the dough is the right consistency, and put it onto a very lightly floured board.

- The ultimate secret to making perfect scones is the kneading — it's all in the hands! I use the heels of my hands to push the dough away from me, then catch it with my fingers and draw it back. It is just as though you were playing basketball: throw-catch, throw-catch.

- Pat it out, shape the sides, and cut it with a big knife. Then onto a baking tray lined with baking paper so you don't have to wash the tray afterwards, and into the oven at 170ºC.

- I cook them until they are firm and nicely coloured. If they expand rapidly like a soufflé, as they often do, I will cut one open when they look as though they are done, just to see if it is cooked all the way through. Everyone's oven is different, and so you have to practise a few times until you get the knack of knowing exactly when they are cooked to perfection.

- Do a lot of catch-and-throw practice.

The recipe

Makes 12 very large scones

6 heaped cups plain flour
4 heaped tsp cream of tartar
2 heaped tsp baking soda
300 ml cream
900 ml full cream milk

Preheat the oven to 170°C. Sift the dry ingredients into a large mixing bowl. Add any additional ingredients at this point. Add the cream and milk. Gently mix with a dinner knife to avoid overworking the dough. When ingredients are almost mixed together, turn out onto a lightly floured board. Using the heels of your hand, throw and catch the dough gently until the dough feels right. The trick is to barely handle it. Then lightly press down to 5 cm thick, and cut into 12 pieces with a floured knife.

Place on a baking tray lined with baking paper, and bake for 15–20 minutes, until golden brown and cooked in the centre. Remove from oven and allow to rest for 10 minutes before serving.

Variations:

Pinwheels

Use the plain scone mixture, technique and temperature for baking.

With a rolling pin, roll out the dough to a large oblong shape, then spread the surface generously with soft butter to the edges. Sprinkle generously with brown sugar and powdered cinnamon. Shake handfuls of currants over the mixture.

Wet the edges and roll tightly lengthways. Cut into pieces half the length of your index finger, and place on a baking tray lined with baking paper. Bake for 15–20 minutes or until golden brown.

Deep-fried Scones

Use the plain scone mixture and technique.

Cut the dough into rounds with a biscuit cutter. Poke a finger into the middle of each round to make a hole. Slide the rounds into a deep pot of medium–hot oil. Cook until brown, then flip the scone over and cook the other side.

Roll in castor sugar with cinnamon. Cut in half horizontally when cool, and serve with whipped cream and Dot's berry jam.

No good for the figure!

Savoury Scones

Use the plain scone mixture, technique and temperature for baking.

Grate a finger length from a block of tasty cheese. Add a large onion, finely chopped, and chopped parsley, thyme and chives. Once mixed, sprinkle extra grated cheese on top. Place on a baking tray lined with baking paper, and bake until golden brown.

Date and Orange Scones

Use the plain scone mixture, technique and temperature for baking.

Chop 2 large handfuls of dates, and add, with the zest and juice of 2 sweet oranges, to the original scone recipe. Place on a baking tray lined with baking paper, and bake until golden brown.

Scones from the family recipe book.

© Fiona Andersen

Rhubarb and Ginger Jam

Makes 6 jars

1 kg rhubarb stalks, cut into 2.5 cm pieces
1 kg sugar
50 g preserved ginger, finely sliced
juice of 1 lemon

Toss the rhubarb in the sugar, and leave overnight to release juices.

Next day, bring the rhubarb to the boil with the ginger and lemon. Boil to setting point. (To see how to test for the setting point, see the Red As Her Hair Jelly recipe on page158.)

Ladle into sterilised jars and seal with sterilised lids, immediately.

Rhubarb forcers in
Dot's garden.

CHAPTER 7

No More Live Presents!

My first job every morning is feeding the poultry. I love chooks. They scuttle around me, squabbling and chirruping as I empty the contents of the scrap buckets about the run. When we started building the restaurant, there was a vacant piece of farmland to the south of the site, and I said to Bevan, 'We'll just make this into a little hen run.'

By the time we had measured it out and got the netting up, in true Smith fashion it was about 50 m long and almost as wide.

I wanted the hens to be able to range as freely as possible, while keeping them out of the garden beds. And I wanted them to live in a warm and comfortable henhouse that looked appealing to the people coming to the restaurant, so I dipped into one of my favourite books, which is about Prince Charles's gardens at Highgrove, and which includes photographs of his beautiful, spacious henhouses.

Our hens, I decided, would live in their own Cluckingham

Palace. I hired Benny Stevenson, and told him exactly what I wanted. Then Neil and I went off to a holiday in Australia. When we came back Benny had built half the chook house, but it wasn't as I had expected it to be. Prince Charles's chook house was like an ornate chalet with a peaked roof covered in shingles, and it had a door that allowed you to walk in, collect the eggs and clean out the old straw and droppings. Benny had built me a doll's house and I couldn't get into it.

It was very cute. It had all the little shingles on the roof, but his perception of size was quite different from mine. We had to put poles into the ground and a platform on top of the poles with the chook house resting on top before I could get into it. No matter. Almost every day someone or other will ask for the design plans so they can build one themselves. The answer is, of course: save your money and hire a builder — don't ask your husband, because he'll take ages to get around to doing it.

Bevan and Monique like to give me live presents. About six years ago, Bevan said to me, 'Mum, come and have a look. We've got you a Christmas present.' Be cautious if anyone asks you to come out and see your Christmas present, because it means it can't fit under the tree and you can't get a ribbon on it.

He took me over to the bird aviary that was ready and waiting for parrots and budgies, and there I found two peacocks. It was not the surprise I had been hoping for. Mr Peacock put his tail out to entice Mrs Peacock to be a mother, and his magnificent feathers touched both sides of the enclosure. Eventually she laid eggs and I decided I couldn't keep them in there any longer, so we built a peacock pen next to the chook pen.

When one of our far neighbours, the glamorous Wendy Bailey, came for dinner one night, she said to me, 'Dot, you've got this gorgeous big peacock pen. I've got a peahen with five babies and I would dearly love to bring them down to join your two peacocks because they're wrecking my garden and I can't keep them under control.'

One of my glamour boys.

So Wendy loaded her six peacocks into a horse float and brought them here to join my two peacocks, and we've had many little peacocks ever since. We don't eat their eggs, but they look magnificent and act as burglar alarms, yelling 'Oi Oi Oi' when they're disturbed. They know me well now and are usually quiet, so they are no trouble. We have got a stable population of 10, and when they hatch their young we give them away so we can keep the numbers down. We also have a pair of colourful pheasants — more presents from Bevan and Monique.

Our aviaries are a great attraction for people visiting Riverstone. After I had bought my first few budgies, people started giving me birds, because they reasoned that I had plenty of room and the novelty had worn off their keeping birds at home. Cath Edmonston, who works with me in the home garden, had a pair of green ring-neck parrots that produced nestlings, which duly arrived in the Riverstone aviary. After two or three generations we have about 14 colourful ring-necks. And we have any number of budgies. The children who come to visit love watching the birds being fed peanuts, grains and lots of veges that have gone to seed.

Another annual celebration, another live present. Mon and Bevan were living down the road and they said, 'Come and get your birthday present', and I thought, 'No! Not another thing that I have to go and get.' But for some reason Neil was very excited about going to see whatever it was, and the grandkids were jumping out of their skin. They had found it on TradeMe and had been all the way to Christchurch to get it.

The silver-crested cockatoo was actually Neil's birthday present to me. It had been hand-reared and was just like a child. All it wanted to do was sleep on my chest with its head tucked into my armpit, and it would make a little cooing sound — ooooooo oooooooooooo — and I would have to pat it. When we got home that night, I had the bird nestled up on my chest and the cat wedged between my elbow and thigh,

Neilly Boy, my gardening
companion.

so I had no room to move. I was like a prisoner sitting in the chair trying to watch something on the television. I was so overwhelmed that I had tears rolling down my cheeks.

Neil thought they were tears of joy, but I was thinking, 'Oh my God, not a *parrot*. I know they live to be a hundred. What the hell am I going to do with a parrot when I'm 99 and the parrot is only 45?' I called him Neilly Boy because Neil gave him to me, and I figured for a hundred years he'd be called after my husband.

Neil said, 'You can't call a parrot Neilly Boy!'

I said, 'Of course we can. You *bought* him!'

We put Neilly Boy in a cage at night inside the back door, and during the day I would let him out and he would sit in the trees around the section or he would ride everywhere on my shoulder. We thought he was hilarious when he repeated our phrases and mimicked our voices. He'd imitate Neil saying, 'Hi, guys!' and 'Never better!'

Then when Neil would come in at night, he would run the bath and Neilly Boy would waddle up to the bathroom yelling 'Had a good day? Had a good day?', and I'd think 'I don't sound like that, do I?'

He was absolutely devoted to me. I would give him his dinner, and he would try to steal anything else he could find in the kitchen — fruit in the bowl, the ingredients for the night's meal. He would stand on the floor beside my feet and talk to me as I was cooking the meal: 'Hello! Hello! Had a good day?' Then he would waddle into the dinette and chew big hunks out of the chair legs and I'd want to throttle him, but he managed to get around me because he was so endearingly funny. He became part of our family, and I grew to love him even though I didn't want to.

At about four o'clock every afternoon, after the parrot had been up in the trees all day, I would go out there and call, 'Neilly Boy, come on down', and he'd yell back, 'Neilly Boy — comin' down', but he would stay exactly where he was. The routine was that I would get the long-handled brush that we washed the house with and stick it up the tree. He would hop onto the brush, and then I'd bring him down. As soon as he got to head-height, he would step off the brush so he could ride on my shoulder all the way into the house.

Then one day Neil went to call him down out of the trees tops. 'Come on, Neilly Boy. I'm in a hurry — come on down.' He replied, 'Neilly Boy — comin' down', and he came right down to the ground. Neil went off to do a couple of jobs, but when he came back he found Neilly Boy lying on the ground. He had climbed up the guide wires, electrocuted himself and dropped dead. It was a very sad day. He is still in the deep freeze in a box, and Neil thinks he is going to have him stuffed and I will stick him in a dome, on a branch. In the castle.

We have another parrot now: George. He had lived for years in a small concrete cage with a mesh front in the Oamaru Public Gardens. He had never been handled, and God he was a vicious bird. Whenever I opened the gate to feed him, he was frighteningly aggressive, squawking and flying at me. It was terrible. I have had him about four years now and he is quieting down, but he has eaten nearly all the noggings out of his cage. I had little parrots in with him, which he really loved, but the parrots used to hop in and out of the corrugated iron because he had eaten all the boards away, so we had to take the birds out. He now lives in his own cage right next to the other birds.

I feed them seeds, fruit and berries and lots of greens. They love corn on the cob. I let the garden veges go to seed because the canaries and finches love the seed-heads. So often people come to the garden and ask why everything is going to seed, and the fact is that we recycle everything and give all the birds the opportunity of having the things that they would have if they were left in the wild.

Another Christmas, another call from Bevan and Monique: 'We've got a present organised for you, Mum, but we're going to take you to Kakanui to get it.' Kakanui is a little beach settlement about 15 minutes south of Oamaru. I thought, 'Thank God. It's going to be a lovely willow basket from Mike.' Mike Lilian, the willow-weaver, has a property out there. I was so excited and I got into the car with great anticipation, and then we headed up to Five Forks, and I thought, 'My goodness me, this is a funny way round to Mike's.'

We headed up a driveway, and Mon said, 'There are some beautiful goats here for you, Mum.'

And I thought, 'Oh my God! What the heck am I going to do with goats? I haven't got any area for them, and they are notorious for eating all your vegetables and trees, and climbing fences and jumping out of gates!'

They were certainly beautiful Boer goats, with cream and brown markings and long floppy brown ears. The two that had been chosen for me weren't that friendly. They were tied up in the barn, but they weren't little goats that ran up to you and said, 'Love me to death.' They were goats that pulled on the end of their tethers and stamped their feet.

I was saying, 'Oooh, this isn't a good sign. I'm not sure how we're going to work this one.' The goat people also had kune kune pigs, and I said to Bevan, 'I think I really like the kune kunes.'

He said, 'Oh well, we'll get them next time.'

When it was time to go home, we loaded the goats into the back seat of the car and I hung onto them, patting them to try to get them under control. Once we had arrived, I suggested to Bevan that we should tie them up in the barn with some straw to let them calm down. We could go and feed them there for a few days and let them get used to us. But no, in his great wisdom he said, 'Mum, we'll just let them out into the chook run where they'll have tons of grass, and they'll be fine.' So he opened the door and got them into the chook run as easy as anything. Too easy. Within five minutes they had chewed all

© Linda Townsend

Why don't they go as fast
on the way out as on the
way back?

my brand-new $35 plum trees down to the ground.

The goats became very friendly, and they were a big part of the chook run for several years. We built a cute little goat house up on poles to match the chook house, and they used to sunbathe on their veranda. But Cath and I would have to lead them out of their enclosure with ropes and chains to feed them each day, and they didn't like the change in their routine. It made them very stroppy and difficult to handle. Their main objective was to home in on my new native shrubs near the restaurant, so we would be hauling and dragging them while patrons and visitors looked askance. The performance certainly wasn't the leading and handling we'd been taught at calf club. We'd be hanging on for grim death while they bolted home, dragging us behind them until they got to the gate of the enclosure. They became so difficult that when Neil and I were on holiday no one else could handle them, and they had to be sent to the great goat farm in the sky.

Hornbeam edging.

CHAPTER 8

Green Fingers

North Otago is blessed with a quality of light that we don't have in the North Island. The first thing I noticed when I came to live here was a clear daylight that seemed to give everything a sharper outline. I know artists and photographers who comment on it, but I'm not sure of its explanation.

Some people say it's the lack of pollution in the air; others put it down to the hole in the ozone layer or the light bouncing off the snow on the mountains. Whatever the cause, Neil and I often notice it. 'Look at the light,' he'll say, just as evening is coming on and there is a pale glow on everything.

The weather, hot or cold, is not as harsh here as it is a little further inland, so you can grow things that you shouldn't be able to grow in this area. It might sound a bit mystical, but I believe the light plays a part in what I have been able to do in the Riverstone gardens.

Even though I have kept a garden since I was five years old,

The September 10th big wind
storm — the wall falls out.

The wall falls in.

Blackcurrants by the ute-full.

Wild pickings for elderberry
and apple jelly.

Berries for jam, clockwise from top
left: black raspberries, karakaberries,
strawberries, boysenberries.

Dot's garden.

Prince Charles and one of his aides
chatting to Ann, Sarah and Dot at
Edinburgh Botanical Gardens.

Springtime tulips
in Dot's garden.

Haymaking Italian style in Milan.

The sweet smell of perfect hay.

© Adrienne Borrie

Sharing my lollipops at the
Himba Village in Namibia.

Two worlds apart — Heron
tribal women.

Not Everybody Can Be The Queen...
Some Of You Have To Sit
On The Curb And Wave As I Go By

Love from Dot . . .

Profusion of summer.

I have learnt so much more since Bevan and Monique opened the restaurant in 2006. In the beginning I would grow any vegetable or herb that took my fancy just because it looked good in the garden, and Bevan would say, 'What on earth do you expect me to do with this?'

'Well,' I'd say, 'you're the chef, I'm just the gardener. I've produced this, so you'll have to find a dish for it.'

He would say, 'Mum, it doesn't work like that. I've got my menus planned. I know what I want, and that's not part of it.'

We have both changed our ways over the years. If I grow things that he is not quite sure about — like yams — he will special them on the menu. Bevan has never liked yams. *I* have never liked yams. I always thought they were watery compared with the kumaras I grew in Northland, and they choke any bed they are planted in. However, their foliage looks fantastic in the garden, so I planted them in a collection of lovely lime-green buckets and placed them along the garden path. They grew prodigiously, and at the end of the autumn I said to Bevan — several times — 'You know, the yams are ready. Do you think you would like to use them?' He'd sigh. 'No, Mum. You know what I think about yams.' I dug them up and delivered them to the restaurant, saying, 'You are going to have to try to use these.' So he came up with a recipe, and it was so popular with the patrons that he ended up ordering barrow-loads of yams from local growers to satisfy the demand.

Then came the Jerusalem artichokes. Fart material, everyone called them. But now Bevan makes soup with them or serves them roasted. I love growing them because they look like giant sunflowers, and they grow exceptionally well in my gravely soil with a bit of cow manure dug in. So Bevan has learnt to cook things that he probably wouldn't have cooked a while ago, and I am learning to do what I am told for the most part, and grow more of what he wants rather than what I think he needs. We now work out what is wanted in advance so that I can have it ready on time. It is like being a market gardener with no soil.

Before he and Monique started building the restaurant, Bevan and I put in the herb and vegetable plots on the south side of the site to supply most of the greens for the kitchen. We built two raised beds measuring 40 m x 5 m, with a wide access path in the middle so that we could get the ute between them to offload the straw and manure from the calf sheds, as well as the manure from the dairy-shed effluent basins. I don't know where we would be without the cow manure. It makes the plants bush up and jump out of the ground. An overhead sprinkler system waters the garden beds, while a trellis abutting the big poplar trees behind them filters the wind so that those garden beds are much warmer than the others around the property.

When I look at the garden I don't see rows of vegetables: I see the colours and textures as much as I see something that Bevan wants. I like to plant flowers with the vegetables to add colour, texture and a touch of real beauty: a border of cabbages back-planted with red roses and the flowers of the elephant garlic plants; dense drifts of poppies give the vegetable beds a splash of colour for a few weeks. The delicate green clouds of fennel foliage look gorgeous with their fat white bulbs.

I plant calendula and borage in the vegetable plots, so that the chefs can use the bright yellow and blue petals for a burst of colour in their salads. And there is something about the look of a row of red cabbages that lifts my spirits. I love to balance their solid, round strength and flouncing outer leaves with the delicacy of rainbow chard and red-stemmed silverbeet, especially when the sunlight makes the chard and beet stems glow red and yellow.

It is important to keep a garden plan so that you can rotate the positions of root and leafy vegetables every year. This helps you manage soil fertility and reduce problems with diseases and insects that live in the soil. While we can't supply all our own needs, we keep about 30 hens to help supply the

Slow-roasted Pork with Jerusalem Artichoke Purée, Winter Greens and Herb Oil

Here is what Bevan came up with to humour me over my Jerusalem artichokes.

Serves 4

1 kg fresh pork shoulder, bone removed
1 tsp sea salt
1 pinch of dried chilli flakes
1 tsp fennel seeds, roasted
4 cloves garlic, peeled and roughly chopped
50 ml olive oil
1 recipe Jerusalem artichoke purée (see opposite page)
4 cups winter greens (kale, cavolo nero, chard)
1 recipe herb oil (see opposite page)
150 ml jus (optional)

Preheat the oven to 200°C. To prepare the pork, score the skin with a very sharp knife. Crush the salt, chilli flakes and fennel seeds in a mortar and pestle. Add the garlic and grind to a smooth paste. Muddle with the oil, and smear the spice mix all over the skin and the flesh of the pork. Place into a roasting dish with 6 cm to 10 cm sides, and cook for 30 minutes. Remove the pork from the oven, add half a cup of water to the roasting dish, and cover with foil. Reduce the oven to 150°C degrees, before returning the pork to the oven and cooking for a further 2.5 hours, or until the meat is falling apart. Remove from the oven and allow to rest for at least 15 minutes before serving.

Warm up the purée in a medium-sized pot. Briefly blanch the greens in a large pot of lightly salted boiling water and drain. Divide the purée and greens between four plates. Remove the skin and excess fat from the pork shoulder and place on top of the greens. Drizzle with herb oil, and a little jus if desired.

Jerusalem Artichoke Purée

1.2 kg Jerusalem artichokes
1 litre milk
200 ml cream
sea salt and pepper, to taste

Peel the artichokes with a sharp knife and place into a bowl of lightly salted water. Drain and place into a medium-sized pot and cover with the milk. Place a piece of baking paper over the milk in the pot. Bring to a simmer and cook for 15 to 20 minutes, or until tender. Strain the artichokes and reserve the liquid. Bring the cream to the boil in a small pot. Liquidise the artichokes in a blender until smooth, and add the cream. Adjust the consistency with a little more of the reserved cooking liquor as required. Season to taste.

Herb Oil

1 cup Italian parsley
2 tbsp fresh thyme
½ tbsp sea salt
1 clove garlic, peeled
½ cup extra virgin olive oil

Place the parsley, thyme and salt into a mortar and grind to a smooth paste. Add the garlic and crush until smooth. Add the oil and muddle to combine.

Our farm workers building
24 new garden beds — the
price of success.

Success after the steam bath.

restaurant with free-range eggs. They live in Cluckingham Palace in a large enclosure and thrive on the scraps from the kitchen and discarded vegetables from the garden.

I had planted the first orchard with a pick and crowbar to get into the gravel beds, shortly after we arrived in the Waitaki, and the old heritage apples, pears, quince and apricots are still there. A few years ago we put in a second orchard of 50 cherries rescued from a local grower who was pulling out his trees.

We get bees in to pollinate the cherries when they are blossoming. Our bee man is Nathan Davis, who runs a business called Treehugger Organic at St Andrews, about 30 minutes north of Riverstone. He places his hives among the trees, and comes down to feed them sugar and water, as there is not enough food for them when the cherries come into flower. So we get his bees for the season and he takes his payment in meals at the restaurant as a barter.

I coped with the garden pretty well by myself until 2010, but I had to employ another part-time gardener to help me after the *Cuisine* award brought an influx of new patrons. We didn't have the infrastructure to deal with the additional numbers, and needed so much more of everything instantly. And I mean instantly. The day after the results were announced, droves of people arrived to try out the restaurant, and I said to Neil, 'We'll have to put in more vegetable beds.'

That day, with the help of Mark Fallen, who works for Neil and me on the farm, I measured up a grid on the stretch of lawn on the southwest side of the restaurant beyond the car park. We had room for 24 beds, each measuring 4 sq m. Again, I needed to be able to drive the ute up and down the middle, and between the beds on the cross-line of the grid, so that we could replenish the beds with compost and take away the old veges. We got in some of the farm workers to help build the raised boxes, each about two hand-spans high, raided the farm's compost heaps of aged cow manure, straw and sawdust, and dumped it all into the new beds.

Then I got Alliance freezing works at Pukeuri to deliver two truckloads of their rich compost made from the intestines, blood and bones of the slaughtered animals, and we put it on top of all the beds. It looked so spectacularly black and rich that I couldn't wait to get the plants in. We'd raised them from seeds, and had enough trays to fill the beds.

It was a good day's work, I thought; but as I stood there admiring the little seedlings in their new beds, I noticed a few wisps of steam curling up from the rich, black Pukeuri compost. Very soon the little wisps became tall plumes of steam. The compost was cooking my seedlings! The next day they were limp, browning and clearly dying, because the mix was too fresh and raw. I had to dig over the 24 beds to blend the black compost with the lower layers of straw, sawdust and manure, and the next batch of seedlings zoomed out of the ground as though they had a bolt of lightning under them.

Leigh Steel, who worked with me in the Regent Florist business, came to help me in the garden. She is a fastidious little person who is an ace at growing things from seed and pricking out the seedlings. And she is no slouch at loading the little tractor Neil bought for us in China, and hauling the compost around the garden beds.

Leigh and I follow the Planting by the Moon calendar at the back of the *NZ Gardener* magazine and get fantastic results. We think the editor is doing a remarkable job. We sit down and read the whole magazine when it comes out every month, and always learn something new, but the calendar is a must. That system, combined with our fabulous cow manure, makes the herbs and vegetables healthy and vigorous.

We don't use anything artificial or chemical on the soil and food plants. Without the cow manure to make compost for all of the veges that we grow, life would be a lot more difficult, though. Every time we water the gardens, the cow manure that we have put on the ground liquefies and feeds the plants. The more you feed plants, the less stressed they get, so you rarely need preventative sprays.

However, we do use copper and trace element sprays on the fruit trees, as these are good for the consumer as well as the plant. If we have to spray the veges, we use a product made from garlic, chilli and pyrethrum that we get from one of the local organic growers, and it really deals to white butterfly caterpillars. I have to weed-spray edges and paths and roads to keep the place tidy, but we put nothing around the food plants.

Leigh and I mass-plant micro greens for the restaurant. We tried different systems, but now we just sow whole packets of seeds directly into the ground, cover them with little plastic cloches, and we can grow what we need all year round. We do the same with Italian parsley, and keep the restaurant supplied throughout the winter. Once spring comes, we fill the tunnel house with basil and heirloom cherry tomatoes that we pick daily for the kitchen staff to pop into the salads. We have also found that by planning ahead and placing little cloches made out of plastic and wire over the zucchini, broad beans, French beans and salanova lettuce in the garden beds, we can harvest them up to six weeks before they are ready anywhere else in the area.

No matter how hard we work in the vegetable gardens, we simply can't supply all the produce for the restaurant. All the food, including the meat and salmon, is simple, natural and traceable, and Bevan relies on local growers for the big volumes of root vegetables that are among the signature ingredients in his dishes. He sources the staples on his menu — Florence fennel, celeriac, carrots and beetroot — from Brydone Growers, an organic market garden at Totara five minutes south of Oamaru, while all our Agria potatoes come from the Bruce family at Willowbridge just over the Waitaki River.

Roast Balsamic Onion and Beetroot Salad with Goat's Curd

Next time you are at Riverstone Kitchen, try the dish below. It is one of Bevan's most popular salads.

Serves 4

10 brown onions
½ cup vegetable oil
1 pinch of ground chilli flakes
½ cup mint, finely chopped
¼ cup standard balsamic vinegar
½ cup olive oil
12 baby or 8 golfball-sized beetroot
sea salt and pepper
160 g fresh goat's curd
salad greens, to serve
extra virgin olive oil
quality aged balsamic vinegar

Preheat the oven to 200°C. Slice off the ends of the onions carefully with a sharp knife. Slice, with skins still on, into thick rings about 2.5 cm thick. Place the onions evenly onto a roasting tray lined with baking paper, drizzle with vegetable oil and roast until extremely dark in colour, even slightly burnt. (The more coloured the onions are, the better the flavour and texture.) When cooked, remove the onions from the oven, and discard the skins and tough outer layers. Toss the onions in a bowl with the chilli flakes, mint, balsamic vinegar and olive oil. Set aside for later use.

Roast or boil the beetroot until tender. Allow to cool just enough so that you are able to remove skins with your fingers. Lightly season with a little salt and pepper, and place on a tray with the roast onions. Warm in oven, and then divide beetroot and onions between four plates.

Crumble the goat's curd over the top, scatter with salad greens, and drizzle with some aged balsamic and extra virgin olive oil to finish. Serve immediately.

© Fiona Andersen

Bevan harvesting greens
from the kitchen garden.

Gluten-free Carrot Patties

This simple recipe fills me up when I am hungry!

    2 cups mashed Agria potatoes
    1 medium-sized onion, finely chopped
    1 carrot, grated
    1 cup grated cheese
    1 egg
    gluten-free flour to thicken mixture
    salt and pepper, to season
    olive oil

Mix all of the ingredients together — except olive oil — with a fork. Form into patties, coat with gluten free flour and fry in a little olive oil, until lightly browned and crisp. Serve hot. Makes six large patties or eight small ones.

© Fiona Andersen

Fresh is best.

When you're strolling around the gardens at Riverstone these days, it's hard to believe that the land was a stark, grey gravel pit when we arrived in 1983. My first job was to build up the soil on the east side of the house and plant conifers to give us some privacy from the main road and the railway line that runs on the far side of it. I would be toiling away there and the train drivers would wave and toot to me when they went past. Every now and again one would drive his car into the property to say, 'It's me that's tooting', and before the conifers grew to be as tall as they are now we did a lot of tooting and waving on both sides of the main road.

The garden has been transformed over the years. Each year throughout the 1980s I developed another area, and slowly worked my way around the section. I planted a tussock garden on the west side of the house because I'd never seen them and thought they were beautiful. I would go to the nursery and buy what they were using for reclamation work. Almost no one in North Otago grew tussocks in home gardens at that time, and by then I was hosting garden walks. The members of various women's institutes wanted to meet the lady who was trying to create a garden on the top of a hill with no soil. I would be quietly walking behind them, and I would hear them saying, 'Goodness me, fancy planting grasses — I don't like *that*.'

A wide bed of flaxes took up the south side of the section. They didn't mind my gravel at all, so long as I put the hoses on and gave them plenty of water. When the tussocks and flaxes grew too big, we ripped them out and I planted the flowers that were the foundation of my first business.

My family is my first love. My garden is my life. It is the only area in my life where I have all the say and total control. Nature dictates the seasons, and we can't change how that occurs, but everything else in the garden is up to us. What incredible power we have in our fingertips! Cath Edmonston has helped me keep control of the home and Pukeuri gardens for the past 16 years. I have always believed that a garden is an artist's palette, so each season we can change the type of plants and colour combinations.

If I use the backdrop colours in the shrubs and trees, I like to make the bedding plants tone in with them. Lime green adds a gorgeous freshness to the mix. My garden is planted in colour areas, and I try to have something in flower throughout the year. I painted the back wall of one of the shops rusty red to give my garden a bold autumn-toned background. It has orange dahlias, fireglow euphorbia, bright orange poppies, lime, orange and red gladioli, bright yellow pansies, and yellow and orange Asiatic lilies.

I painted my grey iron garden seat bright lime last year. It is so pretty and livens up that area of the garden. I added two large lime-green pots beside it, planted with white clematis and under-planted with lemon petunias. Two bamboo obelisks give height to the pots. Clematis grows fantastically well in large pots, because I add new compost to the top each season.

The border has a backdrop of very tall native beech trees, green maples and trimmed topiary totara. In the mid area I have cream and pink rhododendrons, and in the spring the whole garden is pink and lime. Huge clumps of yellow-edged hostas fill the front of the border. It is quite spectacular when everything is up and growing in the early summer. There are massive clumps of yellow Oriental Condor lilies, and each year I buy more lily bulbs. It is so exciting in the late spring to see the fat new shoots coming out of the soils. I put three spades full of my wormy cow manure around the clumps and wait for summer. Some types grow to about 1.8 m, and the air is full of fragrant perfumes in the evening. You would think you had died and gone to heaven.

My garden areas are divided by winding pathways, and our grandchildren love running along them and finding places to play. While Mike had outgrown childhood games by the time we had moved to North Otago, Bevan spent hours when he was growing up playing on the enormous 4-tonne rocks I had placed in what was once the tussock garden. He used to paint little models and create battlegrounds on the rocks with his soldiers. I still sit on those rocks from time to time, and both Mike's and Bevan's children love to climb around them. I put little tables and chairs in other parts of the garden so that the grandchildren can have picnics under the trees. At other times they will play in the treehouse I had built after cutting out the leggy branches in an old conifer.

Cath and I plant wide sweeps of tulips and spring bulbs. At the end of the season we have to lift them, dry them off, then dust them with insecticide and keep them in a dark place for the next spring. I always plant a small patch of Anzac poppies because they remind me of the fields in France and Italy, and Iceland poppies in big groups are my favourites to fill the gaps. Hellebores, trilliums and fritillarias are more spring delights, and the perennial border along the path to the clothesline looks promising in spring, manured, mulched and ready to romp. Last year I made collars for the delphiniums from bracken that I had gathered at the roadside. I tied the collars around big clumps of the plants, then tied the collars to stakes. They worked better than I'd imagined, holding the plants straight and upright.

As I write this, it is nearly Christmas and the perennials have grown into a forest, but the weeds are as tall as the plants. Writing this book has starved me of the minutes I would otherwise snatch to pull them out. We have a deadline looming, but I plan to deal to the weeds before then. There will be a quiet Christmas Day spent weeding and catching up.

I love marble statues, because they age gracefully and look better with time. Many years ago I bought several made in New Zealand by Phoenix Italia. Most people seem to think they add grace to the garden, but one day, when I was hosting a garden tour, I overheard one elderly lady's comment. Upon

Giant garlic flowers — I mix
these through the flower
gardens and reap two rewards.

My favourite gardening tool —
a Japanese hoe.

seeing a Greek god standing in all his manly splendour in a gazebo among the mock orange bushes, she exclaimed, 'Oh, my God — a naked man! I hate naked men at the best of times, and I certainly wouldn't put one in my garden.' I grinned to myself and walked on.

When I came home from my garden tour of Britain in 2012, I decided to make another vege garden in the hen enclosure. I got the farm boys to pick up my beautiful Prince Charles henhouse and move it to the bottom of a stand of trees. It was pretty heavy and it wasn't that easy to pick up, but, with big chains slotted through the little windows, we edged it into its new position without any mishaps. Now I had a whole new area to garden — my secret garden where no chefs are allowed to forage. I wanted to surprise people by planting herbs, flowers, vegetables and Ballerina apple trees in a semi-formal setting. It looks wonderful in summer, with its pathways lined with curly parsley. I have the opportunity to let everything grow without being picked for the restaurant, but when I want to change plantings I can deliver the veges to the kitchen and then replant.

It is a nice space, enjoyed by the visitors, and hopefully it inspires people to try different ways of growing vegetables. I don't believe veges need to be relegated to the back corner of the section — their colours, shapes and textures make them as appealing to the eye as flowers. I love mixing them together. A row of red cabbages and Blackberry standard roses edged with curly parsley makes a great entrance up the garden path.

I plant giant garlic through the flowerbeds. Their flowers are tall and allum-like, and give height and texture to the flowers while keeping aphids at bay, and all the while they are growing big fat corms to harvest in autumn.

While most people the same age as Neil and myself are retiring, we feel we need to make the most of our 50-plus years of experience in farming and gardening. Rather than slowing down, I just find easier ways of doing things, and the exercise keeps me young. My back aches by evening, but I say to myself that this is a sign of achieving a great day's work. My wealth is my health, and a lot of it is mind over matter. I sit in my armchair after dinner and fall asleep.

In the early 1990s, when Neil bought the Pukeuri property as a wintering block for the cows, I plunged into redeeming the grounds there, largely because I thought it would be the site for my castle. The garden had good bones, but we needed to clear away the half-dead macrocarpa hedges and a massive amount of undergrowth. There was an old and very gnarly orchard of heritage pear trees at the back of the house, and several promising rhododendrons, as well as a stand of four huge oak trees that needed the expertise of an arborist to get them back into shape.

Cath and I made a feature of the weeping elm on the front lawn, reinstated the grand old circular driveway, and planted box hedging for structure and shelter. Every time we pruned the buxus we would put the cuttings in pots of sand after dipping the ends in rooting hormone, and waited two years for the new plants to be ready for transplanting. The garden could then look tidy and formal with weekly lawn-mowing and occasional hedge-trimming, weeding and mulching.

We had a lot to deal with, because in that time Cath and I have also tended all the gardens around the houses occupied by our contract farmers, spraying weeds, trimming hedges and mowing lawns every week. The farms have grown in number now, and it is not possible to look after so many gardens, so we have asked the contract milkers to look after their own properties. Neil tidies up if the properties are left unattended to.

My library is full of gardening books. One I turn to often is *The Garden at Highgrove* by Charles, Prince of Wales. I fell in love with the stumpery there, and decided we needed to have one in the Pukeuri garden. First I had a gazebo built, and I put in an avenue of eight marble statues because they remind me of Italy. They are what I see when I look north from the living areas in the house. I had the gazebo placed in the part of the hedge that had died out, persuaded the farm workers to haul in all the old stumps that were lying around the farm, and arranged them around the gazebo. With all this done, I decided that the groundwork had been laid and it was time to get serious about building the castle.

We stock a small selection of garden implements, and I decided to bring in a Japanese hoe from a New Zealand company called Omni. The first time I tried it, I was astounded that I was uprooting small weeds and aerating the soil at lightning speed. It's a small hand-held hoe with an angled blade made from high-carbon steel, and has an incredibly sharp edge and tip. I use it like a little chipper and can get the roots out of docks and clover and those things that are tougher to get out with a trowel. I can whip through all 24 of Bevan's raised beds in just a couple of hours, whereas it would take me a lot longer if I was weeding any other way. I can't think of anything more effective. They've been wonderful Christmas presents, and some people, once they have bought one for themselves, ring up and order six more to give to their friends.

For many years, while looking through English garden magazines, I have loved seeing the big terracotta rhubarb forcers in the vegetable patches. To my knowledge they have never been available here in New Zealand. While on a tour of the great gardens of Britain I took photographs of them on several estates, and once I got home I approached Pottery World in Christchurch, where we buy stock for the shop. They had never heard of them. I showed them my photographs, they made inquiries with a pottery overseas and had a shipment made up for me. The first samples were too small for my big rhubarb plants, but the next shipment of a larger model was very successful and I have been stocking them exclusively ever since.

Pear and Walnut Chutney

This is a great way to use up hard, windfall pears, and is excellent with a cheese board.

Makes 6 jars

- 1.2 kg firm pears
- 225 g tart cooking apples
- 225 g onions
- 450 ml cider vinegar
- 175 g sultanas
- finely grated zest and juice of 1 orange
- 400 g granulated sugar
- 115 g roughly chopped walnuts
- ½ tsp ground cinnamon

Peel and core the fruit, peel and quarter the onions and then chop all into 2.5 cm pieces.

Place in a preserving pan with the vinegar. Slowly bring the mixture to the boil, then reduce the heat and simmer for 40 minutes, stirring occasionally until pieces are tender.

Meanwhile soak sultanas in the orange juice.

Add the sugar, sultanas, orange zest and juice to the pan, and heat until the sugar has dissolved. Simmer for 30–40 minutes or until the chutney is thick and no excess liquid remains. Stir frequently towards the end of cooking, to prevent the ingredients from sticking to the bottom of the pan.

Gently toast the walnuts in a non-stick pan over low heat for five minutes, stirring frequently until lightly coloured. Stir the nuts into the chutney with the cinnamon,

Spoon the chutney into warm, sterilised jars and seal with sterilised lids immediately. Store in a cool, dark place, and leave to mature for at least one month. Use within one year.

© Fiona Andersen

Waiting for the windfalls.

Woven willow draught horse
from UK garden tours.

In the spring when the rhubarb is starting to shoot out of the ground I place the forcers over them and take the lid off. The pots protect the rhubarb from the cold, keep it in the dark, and force the stalks to grow up straight and tall towards the light. The result is soft, red and delicious stems. Bevan bakes it cut into small segments on a flat tray and serves them as a dessert with panna cotta. After a couple of picks you need to take the forcers off, feed the plant with compost, and leave the plant to grow naturally. If you over-force the plants, they become weak and spindly. The forcers then look terrific as a decoration and conversation piece in the garden.

And then there is willow, a material I have come to love. A visit to the willow-weaver Mike Lilian's workshop at Kakanui is like stepping back into a time when craftspeople made a living by their hands and skill alone. Huge bunches of dried willow lean against the walls, and you can see how different willow species dry to blues, greens, pinks and yellow. Mike weaves handmade baskets of all shapes, sizes and uses — picnic, laundry, log, bicycle, blanket, fruit and carry baskets of every kind. The Winchester is designed to carry six bottles of wine.

You will find willow woven chairs, occasional tables and cradles. He even weaves made-to-measure willow caskets for people who want a natural burial. Mike is a tall, handsome man and a great conversationalist. We talk for a while as I watch him using the skills he has learnt over his lifetime. I hope that one day he will teach me at least some of what he knows.

The tour of the great gardens of Britain introduced me to low, woven willow edges along paths, tall obelisks for climbing plants, woven willow walls, and animal structures like draught horses, deer, birds and abstract shapes intricately woven over wire frames. Mike has woven trellises and fences in his own garden, so I asked him to put up a fence of woven live willow to filter the air through the garden of raised beds. It's very effective and is regularly admired by people who visit the gardens, and each spring we cut the top back and strip the new shoots off the growing willow sticks to reveal the woven frame. The live willow grows long leaders aggressively all summer, and Mike has tied these over to form archways. The birds love to nest in the tangly willow branches, and in spring they sport lovely pussy-willow catkins.

Last year Mike made several dried-willow panels to shelter the eight plots of microgreens box gardens from the southerlies. He made a fabulous job and, again, people wandering around often comment on them. I feel it is important to bring new elements into the garden, because so many of our visitors tell us they haven't travelled overseas much, and our gardens inspire them to try new things on their properties.

Pussy willow woven ball in the almond tree.

Every willow weaver has their
own signature. This is Mike
Lilian's.

The live pussy willow lattice
fence to block the southerly
winds.

Sand dunes in Namibia
photographed from the air.

CHAPTER 9

Travel — Recharging the Batteries

Neil and I work seven days a week, for 11 months of the year. During the winter, when the dairy cows have been dried off, we love to get away and travel to somewhere completely different, so that every day off the farm is a new adventure with exotic customs, cultures and landscapes. It recharges our batteries and clears our heads of home issues, and we usually come home with more bright ideas.

Visitors to Riverstone often ask me where I get my inspiration. Really, it is a matter of borrowing imaginative ideas from other people and applying them to our situation. Ideas are everywhere you go if your eyes are open and your mind receptive.

Neil and I were milking 500 cows within the first year or so at Riverstone, and, because dairy farming was such a new industry on the Waitaki Plains, we needed more support than we could find locally. Running a big dairy farm presents different problems and opportunities compared with those faced by one man operating a small herd, so we joined the New Zealand Large Herds Association (NZLHA) and went to dairy conferences where we met people in the same situation. Over the next 20 years we got together at annual conferences throughout New Zealand, and these became the social event of the year on our farming calendar. The Large Herds Association gave us the chance to develop close friendships with other dairy-farming couples, who became like family. We knew their kids, celebrated each other's birthdays and travelled the world together to investigate the farming industry overseas.

Besides investigating farms of different types, the tours always allowed us time to explore tourist attractions in the areas we were visiting, and many of the same people have travelled with us time and again.

Africa

Shelagh Bragg from Te Puke has been the chief sponsor organiser for the NZLHA, and was invited to help establish the South African equivalent. She and her husband, Earl, have invited us and other members of the association to join them on their trips, and we have attended three conferences in different locations in South Africa. We have visited farms around Cape Town and Port Elizabeth, where everything is so different from what we are used to. A big monkey came out of the bush while we were on a farm down on the Garden Route one night. It turned on the switch to the grain auger to help himself to a free feed. Unfortunately for the farmer, the monkey didn't turn the switch off and it powdered a whole silo of grain onto the ground.

We have been billeted with farming families and taken part in the daily lives of our hosts. One day Bev Turner agreed to take us to the AIDS hospital for babies and orphans in the Kwa-Zulu Natal province, where she worked as a caregiver and taught crafts. While the AIDS epidemic was reported widely many years ago, you don't often read about it in the world media these days. But South Africa has the highest prevalence of HIV/AIDS compared with any other country in the world, with 5.6 million people living with HIV, and 270,000 HIV-related deaths recorded in 2011. Our visit to the orphanage was an unforgettable experience.

The matron gave us a talk on the problems surrounding the AIDS issue. During the apartheid years, native African people were relocated to areas out in the country where small settlements had been built to house them, but where there was no infrastructure. There were no jobs, the settlements were miles from the nearest big town and people had to walk miles to the nearest shop.

The men left to work in the mines hundreds of miles away. They had sex with women who could only earn money through prostitution, and the men came home and passed HIV on to their wives. It is a never-ending cycle, as children are born with HIV. The men believed that the women were responsible for carrying AIDS, and many women were brutally beaten, burnt horrendously with boiling paraffin oil and even killed. The child is the ultimate victim in this.

Bev worked as the only white woman in the orphanage, trying to help and teach young mothers a trade or craft to help them earn money. There was very little love for the unwanted babies, which broke our hearts. Rows of orphaned infants lay in cots with no parents left alive, and extended family members too poor to take on another mouth to feed.

Education on how to prevent the spreading of AIDS has gone a long way to help, but the problem is always there.

The high level of security in the farmhouses was another reality we had not experienced before. White farming families are isolated in the rural areas. The houses are surrounded by very high electric fences and gates. Family pets and children are not allowed out of the fenced areas unless supervised. All of the windows of the farmhouses are barred. A grill partitions the hallway so that the bedrooms are secure at night. Coming from New Zealand, we found it difficult to imagine that our lives were at risk on an hourly basis. By law the farmers have to employ local workers, and all of them have to be trained, as they have no experience and limited education.

O
ur eight-seat aircraft made a sweep over the runway near the camp where we were due to spend the night, then climbed back into the sky, made a tight circle, and swooped down again to clear the elephants off the landing field. There are no roads through Botswana's Okavango Delta, so we would fly for up to half an hour from one camp to another. Once we had landed, we were met by a safari tour guide who drove us by Jeep through a stand of trees where the elephants had gathered. Slowly, quietly, we drove through the herd, and watched with surprise as a young male did a mock charge, swinging his trunk, trumpeting and pawing the ground with his huge feet. It was an extraordinary experience.

On our five tours to different parts of Africa, Neil and I have had the opportunity to see the way the wild animal populations are farmed. It is a different Africa from the one you imagined as a child, where the elephants, lions and zebras roam wild on the plains. These days, on thousands of hectares of safari game parks, different animal species are farmed to feed the wild animals on the reserves, and provide a wider gene pool than would be available if the animals in the game

The Reptile and Monkey Reserve on
the outskirts of Johannesburg, where
unwanted pet monkeys and reptiles are
taken. This little fellow just wanted to be
loved. Not good for my hairdo.

parks and reserves were left to interbreed.

Botswana is a very stable country with a population of about 2 million. While most of it is covered by the Kalahari Desert, seasonal flooding from the Angola highlands creates the Okavango Delta, a huge area of swampy lowlands and home to a fabulous range of wildlife. The government of Botswana claimed back all the tribal lands in 1975 and gave the tribal people their own piece of land, where they rear their own cattle and grow vegetables to sustain themselves. They rarely sell their cattle, because their wealth is their stock, not money in the bank. Different farmers also farm zebras, wildebeests, buffalo and lions.

The people in the game park industry who are not farmers have been trained as game wardens and lodge keepers. Tourism plays an important part in this system. The game boys driving tour groups around the game parks every day keep track of what is happening out there. They know exactly how many zebras and wildebeest there are to feed the number of lions and other large carnivores they run. They know where the kill is, and, before too many zebras have been killed and eaten by their predators, they have to be replaced to maintain the numbers. As farmers ourselves, we have been fascinated to see the way this system works, and Neil in particular just can't get enough of Africa. He would go every year if he had the chance.

When we were in Botswana in 2013 it hadn't rained for two and a half years, so it was extremely dry and the game park managers had to fill the waterholes. These are usually located in front of the lodges, so we were able to watch a procession of wild animals coming to drink. The pecking order dictates that the elephants claim the first drink, and they are so clever: even though they live wild in the reserve, they have learnt to put their trunk over the little water inlet and get their share before it has been muddied by the other animals. From the lodge deck, about 15 m from the waterhole, you can watch how the different species interact. The giraffes come down to drink, but if the elephant hasn't finished they wait impatiently on the side. You will see the kudus and other hoofed animals, and you might be lucky enough to spot a leopard hiding behind a dead log, waiting for his chance to pounce.

The waterholes cover about three or four acres, but in the drought they were empty. The water is pumped into concrete troughs big enough for the animals to drink from — and, in the case of the elephants, fire the water over their backs with their trunks — but not big enough to wallow in and make it muddy.

The lodges are like small luxury hotels relocated to the Savannah or the trees or the desert, depending on your destination, and you watch a passing parade of magnificent wildlife and birds coming and going outside your room. For Neil and me it is worth saving every cent we can during the year to put towards experiencing different parts of Africa.

We have also had the opportunity to see the way people live throughout the African continent. Soweto, the black ghetto of Johannesburg, came as a surprise to me. I had always thought of it as a shanty town where black South Africans lived in squalid tin shacks with no running water or sewerage systems. And while that is true for part of the city of more than a million people, there are also Soweto suburbs that have comfortable homes with all the modern city services, and others with luxurious mansions in green and leafy streets.

Nelson Mandela lived in a humble little house in the Soweto suburb of Orlando with his second wife, Winnie, who has converted it into a family museum. While I was there I desperately needed to go to the toilet, and didn't think I could hold on until we could get to a public loo, so the woman looking after the place let me use the one in the house. I didn't think about it at the time, but later I had to smile at the idea of

Neil receiving a sloppy vacuum kiss from one of his best friends.

Riding an elephant off into the bush at Victoria Falls elephant park.

going to Nelson Mandela's place and asking to use the loo, just as though I had been one of the neighbours.

We travelled to Bloemfontein to see the impressive monument to Mandela that had been unveiled on the fiftieth anniversary of his arrest on 6 August 1962 just before he was sent to the prison on Robben Island for 27 years. The sculptor, Marco Cianfanelli, has put together 50 10-m high laser-cut steel poles and placed them on the spot where Mandela was captured. Up close it looks like a forest of steel poles, but when you stand further back the columns come into focus and you can see the image of Nelson Mandela's face.

We stayed the night at a small town called Bethlehem, and wandered down the road to find a restaurant. It had been a long day and we were ready for dinner. We were the only people in the dining room, but the bar next door was buzzing. There was a long wait after we placed our orders, so Earl went next door and chatted with the locals. He brought back a man who was short, had a bad limp and was pretty drunk. After talking All Blacks and where we came from, he asked if we wanted to see some lions the next morning.

We wondered if it was the drink talking, but arranged to meet him at 8am, and then, after an hour and a half, decided we had better find out what was holding up our meal. The kitchen was out of steak and the black waiter had been too afraid to tell us, so he decided to simply act like we weren't there. We re-ordered, got our meals and left to sleep for the night.

At 8am we arrived at the petrol station as arranged with our drunken friend from the night before, and were surprised to find him waiting for us. We followed him out into the country for half an hour until we came to a farm where his girlfriend was rearing lions. There were 72 lions — huge white males and females with very young cubs. The adults were sold to game reserves to improve their gene pool. The lion farmer said we could bottle-feed a litter of cubs. They came out of their shelter very timidly, but feed time is feed time in any animal language, and we were allowed to pick them up and put the bottle in their mouths. They sucked the milk down flat-out, and then snuggled down in our arms. It was a very special experience, and we were extremely lucky to have been given the opportunity as a result of a chance encounter with a complete stranger.

Our travels have taken us to Namibia, where many people still live tribally and as subsistence farmers. The government has established common grazing areas, although some people own a parcel of land. We saw widespread effects of over-grazing. Many of the farmers keep their cattle on the grass verges of the highways because they have no other fodder for their stock. We walked up the mountainous sand dune called Big Mama, with the wind blasting our legs. The view from the top was spectacular, but when I stood still an enormous blue spider appeared out of the hot sand looking to attack my feet. I had to move quickly, then another one appeared and scuttled towards me. I kicked the sand and the spider tumbled down the dune like a ball.

While in Namibia, we were lucky enough to meet a group of Himba women who invite tour groups to see how they live in a little village of round straw-and-mud huts in the bush. The women are the leaders in the community. They avoid anything modern and work hard at keeping their traditions alive. Most of them are tall and slender, with high cheekbones and beautiful eyes. They wear only goatskin loin cloths, and they coat their bodies and their long braided hair in red ochre powder and animal fat. We bought beaded necklaces and bracelets, which they sell to earn an income.

One of the women took us into her hut and showed us how she lived, and through the interpreter explained how she went about her daily chores. These included coating herself in the red ochre — which she did instead of washing herself — cooking meals over a fire and minding the children, who were

A special moment, feeding a
three-week-old lion cub.

Nelson Mandela sculpture on
the site where he was captured
before going to jail.

Elephants in South Africa.

I think the lion cub looks more
comfortable than Neil!

running around with no clothes on. They seemed very happy, healthy and well cared for.

Before we arrived at the village, I asked the guide what we should bring as a present. He said they liked sweet things because they have no sugar in their diet, so I bought a box of lollipops and handed these out to the adults as well as to the children. They loved them! All of the mothers with babies on their breasts were sucking the lollipops, and the little children were sucking theirs and giving them to the babies to suck.

As we were leaving I asked the guide if we could go to the school, and he took us into a small mud hut. There was a blackboard and nothing else. The children sit on the dirt floor, and there was no money for educational materials. Knowing that we would probably find situations like this, we had bought packets of pens before we left Auckland. I went to the bus and collected these and some other things we had brought with us, and the teacher was delighted. It meant that the kids could write.

When we arrived home, one of the women in our group sent a big box of simple educational equipment for the kids in the classroom: paper, watercolour paints, string with pegs so they could put their pictures up to dry; just some of the things we take for granted but they don't have. Many say that you can't do anything for people in poverty, but that is nonsense. For people who have nothing, a little can amount to a great deal.

Sometime after we left the Himba women, we stopped at a roadside stall run by women of the Heron tribe. They wear colourful clothes down to their ankles and headdresses made to represent the horns of their fathers' cattle. These women use an old treadle sewing-machine to stitch colourful little dolls representing themselves in costume, and sell them to earn tourist dollars. Everyone on the bus bought some.

China

R on McPhail of Palmerston North, who specialises in both inbound and outbound agricultural industry tours, has taken us on business trips through Eastern Europe, the United States, the United Kingdom and China.

When we first visited China in 2002 the Chinese dairy industry was in the early stages of development. People in the industry there thought we were an official New Zealand delegation and would set up boardroom meetings, travelling for miles to discuss joint ventures. We had to make it clear that we were just a group of interested farmers and had nothing to offer them.

On one of our trips we visited Harbin, famous in the winter for its ice sculptures. We took the train from Beijing to Harbin in the far north, close to the border of Japan and Russia. We travelled overnight and could hardly sleep because we were so busy looking out the windows as we sped through little villages and vast expanses of country. Harbin's temperatures range from 21°C in summer to -16.8°C, and sometimes as low as -35°C, in winter. The city has hosted the world's biggest ice sculpture competitions since 1985, and the frigid temperatures stop the ice from melting, so the sculptures are on display for a month or more.

Arriving in Harbin at about 7am, we hung onto each other in the crowd as thousands of people jostled and pushed their way from the train platforms, and we were greeted by the night-cart brigade cleaning out the sewage. We were taken to one hotel to have breakfast, but couldn't cope with the menu of 100-year-old eggs, so asked to be taken to a hotel that served Western food. There was another glitch when we had to wait two days to get our luggage from the train. It seems the local custom called for a sweetener, and the men in our group had to give cartons of cigarettes to a railway guard before we could get our luggage back.

Much of our first journey through rural China was like turning the pages in a *National Geographic* magazine. The collective dairy farms near Harbin were like nothing we had ever seen before. The families lived in little houses made of timber and dried cow manure. Each household had two or three fat, sleek cows tethered to posts in the yard. Every cow was considered precious; they were very well cared for, and the farmers would walk them to a communal cowshed in the vicinity twice a day where they were machine-milked. The milk was collected and processed on-site for the fresh milk market. We were fascinated by this way of farming and the way of life the people lived. They were excited to have a group of Kiwi farmers come to see them, and the whole village turned out to study us. I borrowed one of their little black bikes and did a circuit of the village. I thought, 'Well, you're in China, you have to ride a bike! And this might be your only opportunity.' The kids were running around after me, thinking I might not bring it back, and I had to do a lot of waving and grinning to reassure them that I was only going for a little ride.

The main roads in the Chinese provinces we visited were not designed for large motor vehicles, and our bus driver had to ease his way into and out of massive potholes, so the trip was slow, giving us the opportunity to see more of the daily life around us. The more affluent people drove to market on their little tut-tuts with a cage on the back full of live poultry hanging upside down and tied by their feet to the trailer frame. Another form of transport had the Kiwi farmers in fits of laughter. It was a rotary hoe with the hoe removed and a little trailer attached to the back. People also walked long distances to the market, often herding half a dozen sheep. The shepherds carried a stick and wore baseball caps with the peaks swung around to the back.

We stopped at a market where the local people gathered to sell and buy their food. As our bus came to a stop, I suggested we should get out and look around. When several of the group said we had to carry on to our next destination, I said, 'For

Yiwu street traders preparing
their goods.

heaven's sake, we are in the middle of China in a place that you will never see again!', and they agreed that we could stay there for 15 minutes. So Mary Washer and I jumped off the bus, and the people were stepping back because they couldn't believe they had these white people with big noses wandering around in their market so far from a city. We were fascinated by what we saw.

Because they had no refrigeration, people bought their food alive on the hoof and claw, and cooked it fresh at home when they needed it. There were day-old chickens, hens, ducks, goats, pigs, and big bowls of grasshoppers and beetles. They scooped up the insects with a large black ladle and measured them into the people's containers. We were gasping, 'Oh, my God! They're not going to have black beetles for dinner, are they?' A cobbler, with his tools in a large leather pouch spread on the ground, was mending shoes at one little stall, and a tailor sat in the street with his old treadle machine, mending clothes while people waited.

The other members of the tour group started heading out of the little market, but Mary and I were still hanging back trying to take the last photo. When the bus took off, leaving us behind, the Chinese people were distraught. They were yelling and waving their arms, signalling that we should run after the bus, but Mary and I were in fits of laughter. We knew the guys in our group were just having us on, but the people in the market were obviously worried about what they were going to do with us if we couldn't get onto the bus. We walked along, the bus stopped a few metres up the road to let us on, and the market people were all smiles as they waved us on our way.

The *National Geographic*-like images were everywhere. After World War II, the Americans had built the Shanghua Jiang dairy farm in Heilongjiang Province, which consisted of a big brick cowshed surrounded by brick yards, but when we went inside to look at the milking system we found all the machinery in a big heap in the corner. The Chinese farmers had dismantled it, and were milking the cows by hand. That is not the case in China now, of course: their dairy industry is vast and very sophisticated.

Then there was the Peking duck farm. The Chinese have very little animal protein in their diet other than pork, so Peking duck is a popular delicacy. We saw the eggs in the hatcheries — great big bins heated from below by fire. Once the ducklings had hatched, they were put in an enclosed space for a few days before they were transferred to pens for two or three weeks, where the feeding regime meant they grew very quickly. From there they were put into another enclosure and force-fed. A man with his baseball cap on backwards used a stick to herd the ducks into another enclosure. He grabbed hold of a duck by the head, pushed its beak onto a metal spout, pushed his foot down on a pedal and the duck got three big gulps of mash. Then he released the duck and it shook its head, trying to get this stuff down its gullet. The ducks are force-fed twice a day to enlarge their livers.

Later, as we were following a lorry we noticed that it was carrying a tall stack of round cane cages, and in each cage was a small pig. Every now and again the truck would stop, and we would slow down so we could see what was happening. The driver would get out and lift down two or three pigs in their little baskets and put them on the side of the road, and then he would jump back in his truck. He didn't have to worry about putting them in a pen or having somebody there to collect them; these pigs were just delivered to the side of the road and would probably be collected by the farmer or whoever it was who had bought them. Another time we saw an old man riding through a village with two big baskets of eggs on his bike. He would stop at a little wooden house and sell one egg to the house owner. There's a surprise around every corner.

In 1974 a farmer was drilling holes to find water near Xi'an in central-northwest China and uncovered shards of terracotta pottery. He reported his find to the authorities, and within a couple of months a team of Chinese archaeologists began excavating the site. The farmer had discovered a life-sized terracotta army that had been buried with the first Emperor of China more than 2000 years ago to protect him in the afterlife. There are about 8000 terracotta soldiers, from foot-soldiers to generals, in the tomb. They are all life-size, and each one is as different from the others as people are in real life. It is a truly amazing sight to see thousands of clay soldiers lined up, ready for battle alongside full-sized terracotta horses and war chariots. The experts believe it took 700,000 craftsmen and slaves to build the mausoleum, and that they, along with any number of concubines, were killed when it was finished, to keep the mausoleum a secret.

After our group had walked through the buried army museum, in awe at what we were seeing, we went into the souvenir shop and met the farmer who had made the discovery. He was signing books. Later we stopped at a tourism outlet that sold terracotta warriors ranging from 15-cm models to full-scale replicas. I was so inspired by the work done by those hundreds of thousands of craftsmen and slaves 2000 years ago, and so horrified to learn of the way they died, that I needed to have something that would always remind me of their skill and sacrifice. I said to Neil, 'I'm going to buy one of these life-size generals and take him home.' He said, 'Don't be ridiculous. What on earth would you do with it?'

Thinking of the castle I was yet to design, I said, 'I've got the perfect place to put him. I never query when you want to buy a tractor or a piece of machinery, I just take it for granted that you know what you are doing. So you need to take it for granted that I know what I'm doing.' One of the other guys said to me, 'If you buy one, Dot, I'll buy one.' Neil wasn't too happy, but I bought my terracotta warrior and had it shipped home.

You can't travel through this country without visiting the Great Wall of China. Television documentaries, magazine photo spreads, other people's stories — nothing prepares you for the impact of the Great Wall. We could see it in the far distance, snaking over ridges and down valleys — astronauts have seen it from space! Neil and I had seen documentaries about it and were thrilled to be able to set foot there. At the time Neil's knees were in bad shape, and I can still see him climbing backwards down the very steep steps while a monk in orange robes took his photograph.

Once the design for the castle was underway, the next trips to China were devoted to sourcing the right construction materials. We have spent most of our time in the Yiwu markets — the world's largest wholesale market of general merchandise. The market covers well over 4 million sq m, with 62,000 booths inside. From 9am to 5pm nearly every day of the year, more than 100,000 suppliers exhibit 400,000 different kinds of products from cosmetics to construction materials, electronics to sportswear and equipment, hardware to stationery. Because there is no way anyone could find what they need without help, we go to Yiwu with Oamaru businessman Alan McLay, who has strong connections in China, and provides us with guides and translators.

Sarah Scott, our castle architect, has become a close friend to both Neil and me, and she comes with us to oversee the purchases. We spend long hours in these fascinating markets each day, looking at architectural and building components. There are whole streets of marble traders making floor tiles, fireplaces and anything else you can think of. There are streets of lighting — chandeliers of every design and size, from modest teardrops to hotel-foyer size. You will find elaborately carved doors, decorative mouldings, kitchens, flooring, carpets . . .

This was taken at a silkworm
factory where they make
silk duvets.

I love to walk through the back streets near our hotel and watch people cooking traditional food. The vegetable and fruit stalls always fascinate me, because the veges are so different from what we grow at home. The fish are alive in basins of water. The chooks are alive in cages, and the fresh pork is cut up with a big chopper on a wooden chopping block. The range of vegetables is astonishing. The streets are very clean and the people warm and friendly.

Every morning at half past six, Sarah and I would walk around one of the parks close to the hotel. Even at that time of the day, there are hundreds of people taking their morning exercise and socialising on the edge of the large lake bordered by Chinese temples, pagodas and humped bridges. People sit quietly meditating, gambling in very heated card games, or playing traditional Chinese music in the gazebos, while others are ballroom dancing, sword dancing, flying kites on the lakeside, or working as foodsellers and street cleaners.

The object of all this activity in the park is to provide social interaction among the people and keep them healthy. They stretch and extend their legs on little walking machines, and swing on monkey bars to develop their upper-body strength. One man, whom we later learnt was 77 years old, was sliding his left leg up the length of a vertical pole. I was so astonished I turned around and said to Sarah, 'Goodness, I'll have to go and ask him if I can take his photo.' I showed him my camera and asked his permission in sign language. He smiled and nodded and, when I'd taken the photo, a big beaming smile came over his face and he signalled that I should take another shot while he repeated the exercise with his right leg.

One of the most intriguing things we saw was people writing stories on the pavement with huge calligraphy brushes dipped in water. Crowds would gather around to read the stories and poems, and then, when the sun came up, the writing would disappear and the words were gone forever.

Further around the lake, a fisherman was cleaning debris

I just had to have a go, much
to the amusement of the more
supple locals.

from the lake with a net attached to a long pole. I gestured that I would like to take his photograph, but he looked mystified until a woman playing an erhu, a traditional Chinese instrument, explained to him in Chinese and he beamed at me. I positioned him at the lake edge under the willows and grinned at him while making a sweeping gesture around my face to indicate that I wanted him to smile. I thanked him, showed him the photograph on my camera, and we did a lot of nodding and smiling at each other before he trotted away.

The next morning Sarah and I were strolling to the park again when I saw the same man coming towards us across the four-lane highway that runs beside the park. He came straight up to us and made the sweeping gesture around his face that I'd made the day before. I was astonished and appalled to see that he had shaved off his moustache and whiskers! He'd probably had them all his long life. Clearly he thought that's what I had been saying to him — shave your face! He had come to show us what he had done and was obviously happy with it, because everywhere we went that morning he was behind us, smiling and waving.

After our time in Yiwu, we stay in Shanghai overnight before flying back to New Zealand. On our last trip we decided we would like to have a traditional Chinese meal. As we headed towards what looked like an old part of town, a woman approached us several times, asking where we were going, what shops we were looking for. We told her we didn't want to go shopping, we wanted to have dinner. She said, 'OK! I take you. I take you.' We thanked her and said we would find our own dinner, but she persisted until we followed her single-file down a narrow alley, wondering whether our group of eight constituted safety in numbers.

The alley led to a wider street, where she whisked us into a restaurant. Even as we took our seats we were concerned about food poisoning, but the waiters spoke perfect English and offered us a menu written in Chinese characters with coloured photographs of the dishes. Fortunately within a few minutes an Australian man came in with two Chinese women. One of our boys went over and asked, 'Is this a good restaurant?' The Australian said, 'It's the best in Shanghai.' Our man said, 'What are you going to order?' and the Australian said, 'The fish is unbelievable.' So we ordered eight plates of fish.

While the waitress took our order, I asked if I could go to the kitchen. When she looked at me sceptically, I said, 'We've got a restaurant on our farm in New Zealand, and I'd really love to see how a Chinese kitchen works.' So she went away and was gone for about quarter of an hour. I thought, 'That's the end of that. That's a no-no.'

But she came back and crooked her finger at me, saying, 'Come. Follow me.' I followed her downstairs, through a little room filled with tanks of live fish, a different species in each tank. She took me across a small concrete yard and into another building that housed the kitchen, and told me that there were two buildings to make sure that the dining room didn't burn down in the event of a fire from the naked flames under the woks.

Three cooks worked at big woks, sitting on trivets over flames that flared out half a metre. Several kitchen hands worked at a long bench where the orders came in, placing the ingredients for that particular order in front of the cooks. The cooking oil was boiling hot, and I was satisfied that we were going to be quite safe in what we were eating. There was a lot of laughing and pointing at this white woman with the pink hair and the big nose standing in their kitchen, and I laughed with them. After about 20 minutes I went back up to where we were sitting and said, 'Everything's fantastic. We are going to have a great dinner.'

The whole fish came on the plate, complete with head and tail, but they had boned the body, cubed the flesh, coated it with something crunchy and flavoursome, deep-fried it in oil, then ladled on the most delicious sauce I have ever tasted. It was served with rice and stir-fried vegetables, and it was the best Chinese food I have ever eaten. We were all the more delighted because the experience was so unexpected and genuine. And we know where to go the next time we are in Shanghai.

Europe

A couple of years ago, while looking through the travel brochures that come regularly in the mail, my eye was caught by a Flora Garden Tour of Italy and France. I asked Neil if he would like to go. He wasn't that keen, but as we were discussing it a programme came on the television about the Roman Colosseum, and I said, 'Look! That's what you'll be seeing.' I hadn't been to Rome since I was 20, and thought I would love to go back on a tour with everything organised rather than as the penniless traveller I had been in 1968. Neil had never been to France or Italy, so he said, 'Yes, let's go.'

I love these small tour groups. You get to stay right in the heart of the city, and evenings are spent wandering around places where big groups can't go. And a garden tour takes you into the countryside to visit ancient villas and hill-top towns, gardens that lift your heart and ones we couldn't even dream of creating. We soaked up the history and architecture of Florence, Venice, Rome, Milan and Pisa, and travelled up to Lago Maggiore to Isola Bella, where everything had been designed by artists and sculptors and was now so aged that it seemed part of the landscape.

One of the highlights of our trip to Italy was a visit to the beautifully manicured Vatican Gardens. You can only marvel at the statues, flowerbeds, the towering brick wall that also runs through the city of Rome, smaller limestone walls, moss-covered fountains and frescos. One of my precious memories of the Vatican is the white garden with clipped arches of star jasmine spanning a pathway edged in box hedging, leading to a white fountain. The heavenly scent drifted towards me long before I could see it.

We drove through small towns with narrow one-way streets to find the Sacred Wood of Bomarzo, 90 minutes from Rome. The garden was gifted to the wife of the landowner in the sixteenth century, and we wandered among enormous statues carved from limestone — urns, acorns, grotesque faces carved into the rock where you could walk into the mouth and peer out through the eyes. Time seemed to have forgotten this mossy, quiet garden.

We drove through the Tuscan countryside with its fields of sunflowers, grapes and poppies, Cyprus trees and ancient walled villages, finally reaching the medieval town of Bagnaia and the garden at Villa Lante. The first sods were turned here on forested land in the sixteenth century, and the 10-ha garden, built as a hunting lodge for popes and cardinals, is said to be the most complete and perfect example of the Renaissance garden. An abundance of water in fabulous forms cascades from the top of the steep garden in elaborate rills, flows through the centre of an outdoor dining table carved in marble, splashes through fountains and dripping grottoes, and spills into the fountains in an elaborate knot garden at the lowest level.

That visit to Italy has left me with mental images that come to me time and again: lunch at a small café in an eleventh-century village; lanes so tiny that you had to walk through them single-file and almost sideways; ducking your head underneath lintels and stepping through elaborately carved doors; a garden in Sienna with an avenue of lemon trees in enormous terracotta pots that are brought into a barn in winter; masses of roses on old stone walls; hunting lodges and castles. It makes me wonder if people will look at my castle in 500 years and want to know who built it and how.

Star jasmine arches at the
Vatican Gardens. The heavenly
perfume filled the air.

We booked ourselves in for a cooking class one afternoon in Florence, and a mistake in the translation of the class list from English to Italian had Neil described as a chef with a restaurant in New Zealand. When he was given the task of chopping vegetables and helping to cook, I laughed out loud. Neil hasn't lifted a spatula since he left the Army! He was only there for four months and that was 50 years ago when he was doing his National Service. These days he only cooks porridge and toast at home, and is happiest doing the dishes.

In Florence we struck torrential rain: the streets were awash, which made sightseeing difficult. Not deterred, I took off my shoes and ran around barefoot, wrapped in a waterproof poncho and looking like a drowned rat while everyone else was huddled in shops and doorways.

Neil and I thoroughly enjoyed the day we spent walking the Cinque Terre, the five villages on the rugged coast of Liguria. The coastline, the villages and the surrounding hillsides are all part of the Cinque Terre National Park. Over hundreds of years, people have built terraces right up to the clifftops that overlook the Mediterranean. You can't reach the villages by car, but they are connected by paths, trains and boats.

We spent a full day walking up very steep steps cut into hillsides, around goat tracks, through olive groves, and down into villages perched on the side of cliffs where the four-storey houses are painted terracotta, yellow, blue, green and pink, all the while looking down into the deep blue Mediterranean Sea. Manarola clings to the side of the cliffs, its unbelievably narrow streets and phone-booth-size espresso bars crowded with tourists. We huffed and puffed up steep hillsides, through vineyards to Corniglia high on a rocky outcrop.

Vernazza has a castle tower and a beautiful sheltered harbour, where the fishing boats, drawn up on the shore, are the same gelati colours as the houses. The houses of Riomaggiore step down to the water's edge, and Neil peeled off his clothes and sank into the water so that he could say he had swum in the

Mediterranean. I had to hold a towel up for him while he got out of his wet togs and back into his clothes.

We caught the train back to where we had left the rest of our tour group and felt we'd had the better part of the excursion. Even so, we were pretty tired for the next couple of days, and were glad to have a schedule of garden visits to get our energy back. The tour took us to gardens in the gorgeous French countryside — Nice, Avignon and the parfumerie at Grasse. Virtually everywhere, I found inspiration for little nooks and crannies at home.

As we were about to leave Italy, Neil was watching sport on TV in the hotel room near the Milan airport while I went for a walk. I dashed back to the room and said, 'Neil, you must come outside with me — I have just seen the most amazing sight.'

Neil and I walked down the road onto a tiny farm, following a tiny irrigation channel to where a very elderly couple were pitch-forking hay stooks and taking them to a barn in a little hand-cart. The hay smelt sweet and delicious. The lady was crinkled and so tiny that she came up to my chest. I did my mime of asking them if I could take their photograph and they raised their thumbs, smiling and nodding. That night we went back to their house and knocked on the door. The gentleman came out and, with more sign language, I offered them Neil's New Zealand cap and rain jacket and all our leftover powdered chocolate sachets and biscuits.

They gestured for us to come inside and we spent an hour or so discussing the All Blacks and farming in vigorous sign language. I made hot chocolate for all of us, fishing around in the cupboards for a pot. They were so excited that they brought out their family photo album, and we looked through it while we drank the chocolate and ate biscuits. When we said our goodbyes and got up to leave they stood in the doorway, waving and smiling. Neil said the evening was one of his tour highlights.

Australia

Neil and I have wonderful friends in May and Robin Murphy from Glenavy, just 5 km north of Riverstone over the Waitaki River. They are dairy farmers with similar interests to ours, and for many years, when we dried off the cows in June or July, we have taken holidays together. Over the years we have travelled around most of Australia, sometimes with the Swagman's Tour Company through the outback, visiting aboriginal reserves, sheep stations and cattle stations in areas we would call desert. The boys always want to detour up farm tracks to see what's happening, and this way we have visited cotton farms, beef farms, water reticulation dams, fruit farms and coffee plantations.

You haven't lived until you have ridden atop a coffee-picking machine and tried to act as though you are sure that the insects and spiders that land on your head and shoulders from the shaken bushes are not venomous. On one trip we were introduced to Talc Alf, a recluse living hundreds of kilometres from the nearest town. He mines talc rock that is made into talcum powder. As well, he does a bit of carving and hunts kangaroos for the pet-food industry, leaving the carcasses in a cool box for the refrigerated truck to collect whenever it passes. He let us pedal the bike he uses to power his washing machine.

America

You could spend a lifetime in America and never hope to see all of it, and my mind is full of snapshot images from our travels there. We have travelled down both coasts and through the centre of the country for more than three decades with the dairy-farming fraternity, visiting dozens of dairy farms, nearly

One of our favourite days spent
walking the five villages of the
Cinque Terre.

The Baron's present to his
wife: Secret Woods Garden,
Bomarzo, Italy.

Orange grove in a Siena
garden, Italy.

Castle grounds and hunting
woods in Tuscany.

all big cow-barn systems. The men in our group love looking at the machinery, silage stacks and effluent disposal systems. We girls are OK with that, but love to see the homesteads and gardens, and talk with the farmers' wives. Often they turn on barbecue lunches with huge steaks on the grill, and the neighbours dine with us so we can all chat together.

I have never seen so many animals in one place as when we toured the Harris feed-lot where 40,000 cattle are grown out each year on 2 sq km of impeccably clean, enclosed space, for the supermarket trade. Later we ate in their beautiful restaurant that serves the best beef imaginable.

Wherever we go with the Large Herds group, the back seat of our bus is the boardroom where everything is up for discussion — politics, farming practices, employees. Lies are told, short yarns are spun, women's behaviour is analysed, farms are bought over the phone while travelling . . . and that's just the blokes. We girls sit together and have our own conversational topics. Birthdays and wedding anniversaries are always a good excuse for everyone to celebrate.

No matter where you go in the States, there is always another magnificent spectacle to take in: the giant redwoods in California contrast with the wind farms that spread out for miles in every direction, gently rotating to produce clean energy for Los Angeles. We have taken gondola rides from the desert floor at Palm Springs up to the mountain tops where the cable car lets you out onto the snowfields and friendly raccoons greet you, looking for a handout.

On the East Coast, we stopped at a market to see the arts and crafts in the Amish countryside, where the parking area was given over to black horse-drawn carriages with handsome horses waiting patiently. In Florida, we whizzed through the Everglades in shallow-bottomed boats, zooming around swamp trees with their limbs dripping with Spanish moss and their roots exposed above the ground, while crocodiles sunbathed on the banks.

New Orleans was a vibrant and colourful city when we visited a year before Hurricane Katrina. When we returned two years after the cyclone, the people there were still facing the misery and destruction caused when the waters breached the levee, flooded out the homes and destroyed the lives of so many people. I bought a painting at the markets to remind me of the hardships people faced.

We have travelled from the deserts of Arizona, New Mexico, Nevada and Wyoming to the huge grain belts in the northern mid-western states and the southern cotton belt. I stood on a block where slaves were sold into a life of hardship. In Atlanta we took a tour of the CNN newsroom, the Coca Cola headquarters, and civil war battlefields, and stayed in slave quarters and mansion houses. We asked to play the piano in the drawing room of a gracious mansion house, only to be told that it was locked and no one had played it for years. After much persuasion the key was found and one of our group played while we danced and sang half the night. The staff and other visitors came to watch the group of Kiwis having a great time, clapping and singing along with us.

Going to Dollywood and the Dixie Stampede show in the little town of Gatlinburg in the Smoky Mountains was so much fun! What man doesn't want the chance to see Dolly Parton? Her theme park employs more than 3000 local people and, besides offering rides and entertainment, she has employed artisans who are reviving the traditional crafts of wagon-building, leatherwork, woodcarving, glass-blowing, grist-milling and baking. Dolly is a living example of what you can achieve if you follow your dreams. It will probably come as no surprise to know that Neil and I are country and western fans and never miss an opportunity to take in shows at the Grand Ole Opry and other Nashville fixtures.

On a plane ride from Chicago, we landed in a snowstorm in Wisconsin. It was a total white-out. I had to buy some better shoes, as I was wearing sneakers and my feet were frozen

in minutes. The bus drove us out of town to the conference
centre, on a road completely covered in virgin snow, and there
was no sign that there was a road at all except for the road-
markers at the edges. Inside the conference centre everyone
headed for the heated pool except one of the other ladies and
me. We were outside and all rugged-up, making snowmen,
snow dogs and snow cows, and having a snowball-throwing
contest. It was great fun.

In Wisconsin on a different trip, while the guys went off
on a day trip to a university, several of the girls and I went to
see one of the local tourist attractions: Alex Jordan's House
on the Rock. Google it (www.thehouseontherock.com). The
opinions of people who have been there and recorded their
responses to his creation are split between those who think it
is an enormous and fabulous fantasy land — a testament to
the imagination and stamina of an extraordinary man — and
those who think it is the overwhelmingly grotesque work of
a maniac with too much money. I am in the first camp.

Most people regard their dreams as fleeting fantasies,
seldom with substance and rarely achieved. Alex Jordan
had a dream to build a house on the pinnacle of a rock in the
backblocks of Wyoming. He began his project in 1945 and
officially opened the house to paying visitors in 1959. Over
the next 30 years he added rooms, separate buildings and
entire streets of shops to display collections of curiosities
and antiques, including dolls, guns, mechanical musical
instruments and cars. It houses the world's biggest collection
of Bauer and Coble stained-glass lamps, said to be more
valuable than original Tiffany lamps. He built an infinity room
that juts out 66 m from the original house, without supports.
This alone has more than 3000 windows. He built streetscapes
of an early twentieth-century American town. There is an
entire building dedicated to elaborate carousels, and so much
more it would make your head spin. This place has been an
inspiration. It taught me that if you want something enough,

you just go for it and ignore the knockers and naysayers. This man could build a little castle in one day before morning tea!

About 12 years ago Neil and I were returning home after a trip to Arizona with a group of friends. We had a three-day stopover in Fiji, and Neil caught a bug and felt dreadfully sick, so he went to bed. I got my friend May Murphy, who was travelling with us, to put a colour through my hair, and then I sat out in the hot sun, waiting for the dye to take. Neil came out and said, 'Gosh, Dot, have you seen the colour of your hair?' I replied, 'It's OK — it's got another 20 minutes to go yet.'

When the time was up, I went into the shower and washed the dye out and — what a surprise! — my hair was shocking pink all over! Neil and I burst out laughing and couldn't believe our eyes. At dinner in the restaurant, the staff were laughing and asking me what had happened. The air hostesses on the plane were grinning and commenting. I met my sister and our son Michael while we were waiting for the connecting flight to Christchurch, and they were in fits! I was fast becoming a sideshow. I just had to say, 'Never mind. I can't do anything about it now. I'll have to wait until I get home.'

I toned it down with more dye, but I'd had so much fun with pink hair that I decided to keep it in some form or other. It keeps me young. There aren't too many 65-year-olds with pink hair. It has become my signature, and when I go to the trade fairs everyone knows me. Most elegant ladies from the best parts of Auckland wouldn't be seen dead looking like me, but I bet they don't have as much fun as I do.

The Americans love anyone who looks as though they are enjoying themselves and making the most of life, so my hair always starts a conversation. I have had men approach me at hotel breakfast tables to say, 'I love your hair, lady. Where are you from?' I was shopping one day when a woman customer said, 'Can I take your photo? You are *so* colour coordinated!'

It happens nearly every day in the States, and always leads to an exchange of comments about New Zealand and the charms of wherever it is we happen to be visiting.

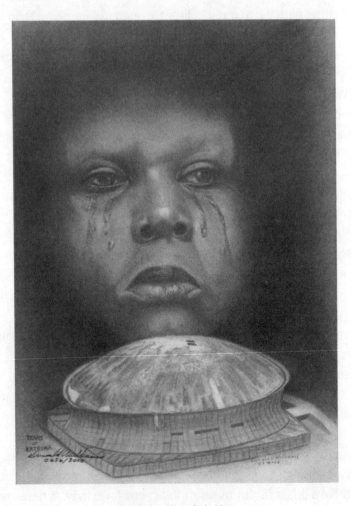

A painting I bought in New Orleans which captured for me the hardships of Katrina.

Great gardens and houses of Britain

By 2012 I had been working closely with Sarah for three years, and we were about to begin the construction work on the castle. I decided that she and I needed to take a tour of the great houses and gardens of Britain to gather more ideas for the castle. Sarah loves telling this story, so I will hand it over to her.

On the first day of the tour we had been strolling in light rain through the Royal Botanic Garden Edinburgh for about 15 minutes when one of the women in our group said, 'Look! There's Prince Charles.' And, sure enough, there was the prince planting a tree, accompanied by two aides, both holding umbrellas. HRH was about 30 m from where we were standing, and we 16 women were peering at him, fascinated by the fact that we were so close to a royal personage. When he had finished what he was doing, he started to walk towards us. As he ambled up, we were all standing there agog and he stopped to chat. Dot, being Dot, immediately engaged him in conversation, and it was all to do with the blimmin' trainers she had bought at The Warehouse.

He said, 'Hello, ladies. Where are you from?'

One of our group said 'Australia!' and I added 'and New Zealand'.

'Oh, you are from the antipodes! Are you on a tour?' One of the others confirmed that we were on a garden tour of Britain.

'Are you coming to Highgrove?' he asked, to which Dot replied, 'We *wish*!'

'Hard luck,' he said, and added: 'It's a bit wet today. You might need gumboots.'

And Dot said, 'Oh, better than gumboots — I've got

these shoes that have got special things in the soles.
They're supposed to make your calves shapely.'

And the Prince just grinned and chuckled. I bet he
hasn't met many people like Dot — pink hair, full of fun
and not at all fazed by talking to a prince. We didn't even
think to curtsy. The rest of us were holding back and being
deferential, but Dot was in there — trainers and all.

Each night while we were on the tour I sent a text to Neil
about the day's activities. That evening I wrote: 'Drizzly.
All well. Met Prince Charles. Off to Drummond Castle
tomorrow.'

Neil replied: 'Pull the other tit.'

Some of the Australian ladies on the tour emailed photos
of the interaction to their local papers back home and it made
front-page news.

Sarah Scott outside Gresgarth
Hall with a dibble used for
planting bulbs. 'I've gotta have
one of these!'

Garden tour group at Hidcote
Manor Gardens.

Silver birch frame
for perennials.

A hotel for insects at Hidcote
Manor Gardens.

Belsay Hall castle ruin.

Riverstone complex from the air — lake and island being created.

CHAPTER 10

How to Build a Castle

I turned 60 in 2008, and said to Neil that it was time to build our little castle while we still had the years ahead of us and the energy to enjoy it. I wasn't planning anything grand; it would be the new home I'd never had, built to look like a castle. The garden at Pukeuri made the perfect setting for what I had in mind — a castellated stone-veneer façade built onto the villa, with an internal courtyard that linked it to an adjoining stone wing.

I'd had a clear idea of what I wanted for 30 years, and I had saved all the money that came my way: most of my earnings, my share of my mother's estate, and the proceeds from selling the shops in town. Most of the money was invested with Hubbard Management Funds and had compounded annually.

I had never taken a cent out because I desperately wanted a castle more than I wanted a new car or to replace the threadbare carpets in our little farmhouse at Riverstone.

I asked everyone I knew in the building industry to recommend an architect, and one name came up more often than any others: Sarah Scott from Wanaka. I found her number, gave her a ring and said, 'You don't know me. My name's Dot Smith, I live in Oamaru and I want to build a castle.'

'Ummmmmmmm,' said the voice on the other end of the phone. We talked for a few minutes and organised a time when she could come to see the Pukeuri property and discuss the possibilities. Three weeks later, when she arrived at Riverstone, Sarah took one look at me with my shocking pink hair and thought, 'My God! What have I got here?' But she obviously enjoyed my enthusiasm as much as I appreciated her sense of humour, intelligence and interest, so we got on like a house on fire. Over the past five years we have become close friends, exploring each other's lives, travelling together, batting ideas around and laughing riotously at each other's take on life.

On the day we first met, I was so excited to think that finally I had the money to be able to make this happen. I said to Sarah, 'This is all the money I have. I can't rob money from Neil or the farms, so it has got to fit within this budget. I don't mind if the interior isn't finished, but we need to get the shell built.' Then I showed her the sketch of the building I had in mind and gave her a box of magazine cuttings I had been putting together since the 1980s. There were hundreds and hundreds of pages of room treatments and finishes, outside and inside details — everything from bedrooms to belvederes.

Sarah went back to Wanaka, drew up the design and made several more trips to see us at Riverstone and to check the Pukeuri site. I would drive over to Wanaka every now and again so we could make changes to the plan. Then, just when she was about to submit the design for the resource consent, the carpet was yanked out from under my feet.

Throughout 2008 and 2009, when investment companies throughout the world were falling over, I was well aware of the possible impact of the global financial crisis here in New Zealand. I made enquiries at our bank about transferring my money from Hubbard Management Fund and a trust. Neil and I discussed it, and he persuaded me to leave my money where it was, because he was concerned that if everyone withdrew their investments it would guarantee a collapse of the New Zealand financial system. When I spoke to Allan Hubbard, he said he would personally guarantee the safety of my savings.

My trust investment, which represented all my shop wages for six years, was due to mature in March 2008. By January that year, when the sharemarkets were in trouble, I applied to pay the last two installments together so that they could pay me out, but was told that it wasn't possible. Bingo! Just what I thought would happen, did happen, and I have had only 10 per cent paid back from my investment. They send me screeds of information on how they think they can trade their way out of trouble and urging me to be patient. It leaves me feeling flabbergasted, just like so many others in a similar situation.

Then, by 2010, the Hubbard Management Fund was in trouble. While Allan Hubbard's South Canterbury Finance company was guaranteed by the government, the Hubbard Management Fund wasn't. Neil and I remained strong supporters of Allan Hubbard, but I had lost most of my money.

When things turn out badly for me, I always go quiet. If Dot's quiet, you know something's wrong. I am usually noisy, boisterous and on top of the world, but when things aren't right I never cry or scream, I just fall apart inside and it takes a bit to kick me back into gear. Neil kept saying to me, 'You can still eat three meals a day. You have still got a roof over your head. You still have more opportunity than anyone else around here, because you are who you are and you'll remake that money in a different way.' He knew how to get me out of feeling sorry for myself, and before long I was saying to myself, 'Of course you can do it. Away you go again, girl!'

However, Neil never seemed to want to live in the house at Pukeuri, even if it was remodelled as a castle. He was happy enough to farm there, but he didn't want to live with the coastal erosion that would see the house fall into the sea within a hundred years or so, and he wasn't keen on living where we would be exposed to the cold southerlies and easterlies whipping off the sea. Besides, Riverstone is the nucleus of our farming operations, and he had to be here every day to work. He had reluctantly gone along with my plan to build the castle on the south side of the Pukeuri villa to block the winds, but I suspect he always thought he would have to come up with a new location. So he woke me up one morning and said, 'I've got a brand-new idea for you, Princess. Come with me and have a look at what I've got in mind,' and he waltzed me outside.

It was very early morning, before anyone else was up and about. I was still in my pyjamas and was hobbling over the stones in my jandals. He told me to look at the boggy old 4-ha paddock in front of the restaurant, and said, 'I think what we could do is build a lake for farm-water storage on that bit of land, so we'd have a backup for irrigation, and I might just build an island out there — and we could put the castle on it. What do you think? If you can visualise that, I'll back you and that's where you can build it.'

At first I wasn't overjoyed: I already had my castle designed, and in my mind I had it built and furnished with the treasures I had been collecting for 30 years. It was a new way of thinking about it, and it meant we would have to have another design. I rang Sarah and said, 'Neil and I have changed our minds.'

She was devastated for a moment, until I said, 'It's not "no", it's "yes" — and it's bigger and better. But we need a whole new design because it is a different location and the castle we have designed won't suit the site.'

So off I went to Wanaka again, and sat with Sarah and Jen

Nelson, her architectural graduate who had grown up in what was originally the forge in the grounds of Glanmore Castle in Ireland. They said, 'What do you want?' I told them I had a lake for a moat and a 60-m diameter island — about a third of a hectare. I said we had a bit more money than what we'd had before, because it now had to be a different style of house, but there wasn't a lot more to play with. However, because it would be in full view of the restaurant and gardens, it had to look impressive from every angle.

We decided the rough perimeter to accommodate the number of rooms we would need, then Jenny threw images of castles onto the computer screen, and as we looked at them, she and Sarah would say, 'What do you like about this one? What do you like about that one?' We borrowed a bit from Leeds Castle, a tower or two from another one, and snipped some elements from my favourite castle, Hever. There was a lot more work to do before the design was finalised, and, as I write, we are still making minor alterations. However, my first priority for the interior was that it had to be warm and comfortable all year round, so insulation was the key.

How do you design a house on a budget? Take your time. I wanted to build a playhouse filled with laughter, music and fun. I have collected things that have taken my fancy from countries all over the world, so everything in the castle will hold wonderful memories. I went through the magazine clippings again, and noticed that the same images and elements were repeated over and over again. I am not modern or minimalistic. I want furniture that has been around, preferably for centuries, with all the knocks and scratches. I could decorate it to define the seasons: old vases filled with spring blossom or winter dogwood branches and birds' nests.

The finished building will be 1150 sq m over three floors. That is the equivalent of 12,000 sq ft, and about the size of four standard modern houses. However, the liveable area is much smaller, because a lot of space is taken up by the towers, the dungeon and the large ramparts — outdoor areas to the east and the west of the top floor.

When we were in the early design stages, everybody was asking, 'Has it got a dungeon? A moat? A drawbridge?' That's all people wanted to know. One of the first things we had to confirm was the type of construction materials we would use. Neil was determined that if we were going to build it, it needed to be solid — it had to be built to last 300, 400, maybe 500 years, otherwise what was the point of building a castle?

So we went for a solid masonry construction, rather than putting it up in pre-cast concrete panels. While Neil let Sarah and me make most of the decisions, there were two things he particularly wanted: a dungeon, and a secret passage that led to the outside of the castle. And because we are building on an island, we had to build the dungeon and the secret passage above the water level, so the ground floor of the castle is a good metre higher than the island.

We had great fun in the design process. Neil and I would come up with an idea, then after a little time had gone past we would think of an alternative, and, unless it was something structural that had to be done in a certain way, Sarah and her team really enjoyed playing with our ideas to see how they could make them work.

On the original plan the secret passage ended in a ladder, and you would have to push a rock aside to get out onto the island, but then, after the construction was already underway, Neil had a brainwave. He decided he wanted to extend the secret passage another 20 m to the edge of the lake, so that he and the grandkids could paddle their kayaks into the entrance. The tunnel is now almost 40 m long, with a series of bends along the way. Neil can kayak to the entrance and, because he's a bit shy at times, he can come inside without having to meet a lot of people when we've

First you have to dig a lake:
scraping topsoil from
the paddock.

Sealing the lake using the
stripped topsoil.

got guests. He will be able to come through the tunnel into the dungeon basement, and then, as well as the main stairs up into the house, there is a secret staircase that leads to an undisclosed location in the castle.

We positioned the house so that the rooms we would be using all the time face north, east and west to capture all-day sun. I wanted a really grand entrance and another one for everyday use. The grand entrance opens into the atrium where the facing wall will serve as a backdrop to a changing feature — sometimes a work of art, on a gigantic Christmas tree or whatever takes my fancy and the season dictates. The formal dining room is the largest room in the castle where we can entertain a small group of people. And it has a fireplace big enough to walk into.

Neil and I have an apartment in one corner of the ground floor: a bedroom, a bathroom, a separate private sitting room where Neil can retreat to watch sport on TV and just have space for himself, and my one great personal indulgence — the dressing room I have never had before. Fancy being able to walk in and find your clothes nicely hung, shoes on racks, and have enough room to get dressed.

There is a large kitchen with an adjoining scullery, and a dining room that leads into a conservatory on the northwest corner to let the sun filter through. French doors lead from there to a large outdoor dining area. The billiards room and table tennis room lead off the formal lounge room, and the rest of the ground floor is given over to staircases up and down to both levels and the utilities: guest toilet facilities, laundry, household storage, the electrical plant room, wheelchair access, Neil's office and the garage.

When you reach the top of the grand stairway a 10-m well spills down into the atrium. Two skylights in the roof above the stairwell let in the natural light, and at the time of writing we have yet to find a translucent, decorative dome beautiful enough to take people's breath away. The first floor has four en suite guest rooms, and a lounge with a view over the lake where people can meet, drink coffee and tea, and use the computer.

Each bedroom has French doors that open onto expansive outdoor living areas, so guests can sit outside and enjoy a glass of wine while they take in the view of the sun setting over the mountains to the west, or the early risers can watch the sun come up behind the restaurant and farmland to the east.

And because we want the castle to have a life long after we have gone, we have had the external areas on the upper floor structurally engineered so that two more guest rooms can be added to each wing. Perhaps it could be used as an eight-room boutique hotel in the future.

When it came to planning the joinery in the rooms, we had the option of trying to get recycled timber beams from Christchurch, but Neil decided to harvest the macrocarpa trees off our farms. I love the fact that they had grown here for a hundred years and more, because, although New Zealand is still a very young country, the wood from those trees brings a sense of history to the castle. And macrocarpa is the most gorgeous hardwood, with a scent that lingers in the house long after it is built. Sarah made up a two-page list of all the sizes and lengths we would need for lintels, ceiling beams, mantelpieces, doorways and interior joinery, and the local sawmiller, Lewis Hore, cut it up for us. He did a fantastic job, and the wood will have had a chance to dry for at least two years by the time we use it.

We will have beautiful exposed macrocarpa beams right throughout the kitchen, dining and family rooms, with deep timber lintels through that area. The billiard room will have lovely timber panelling up to dado level. We have probably got about twice as much wood as we need, but it makes beautiful joinery timber and we will be able to use it for everything from tables to bookshelves and doors, so none of it will be wasted.

I can't wait to dress the windows, because the sills will be more than half a metre deep — perfect for displaying beautiful vases of flowers, blossoms and foliage. We have recessed all the bookcases and cabinetry, which adds to the solidity we get from the plastered masonry internal walls on the ground floor. Everything will have substance. I want people to feel as though they are walking through a castle in England — you can feel the solidity of the walls when you move around a building that has been built to last for centuries. The exterior walls on the top floor will be Oamaru stone, but the interior walls are timber-framed and we'll probably gib those, but we will use some lovely cornice mouldings and gorgeous wallpapers.

The castle is still a work in progress and, although I have had a very strong vision of what it could look like from the start, everyone involved in this project — especially Sarah and I — have spent hours and days batting around endless images and ideas. I know that as the space evolves my thoughts are evolving, too. There are certain things that have been very clear to me right from the beginning of this project, whereas there will be other things that will become new possibilities as the spaces start to take shape. And I have my magic wand at the ready.

While I have an eye for the overall design, Sarah really knows about the structure and construction side of things, so I will get her to tell you about that.

> There was a lot of talk about the structure, and it grew in the three years before we started the construction, but right from the start, when Smithy and I talked about it, he was adamant that the walls needed to be substantial. They are almost half a metre thick, whereas the foundations are nearly a metre thick, because they bear a massive weight. The building itself is made of 200-mm solid, filled concrete blocks. Then thick sheets of polystyrene are attached directly onto the concrete blocks on the outside for insulation, and the exterior will be large bolstered Oamaru stone blocks about 150 mm deep. It is not a cheap

Getting ready for the first
concrete pour.

Loading the site with blocks.
Getting ready for Goldie.

Building the towers using our
ingenious 'cake-tin' form.

form of construction, but it is permanent.

And because this is a big masonry building, it is very important that the heat is contained within. It will take about a year for the concrete to fully dry, by which time it will come up to its optimal room temperature, which will be 18–20°C because of the way we are going to heat it. The structure of the building will be incredibly thermally efficient. It will warm up continually, hold the heat and radiate it, so that Dot and Neil will have even temperatures all year round.

We are using a geothermal system in the lake. There will be hundreds of metres of pipework laid on the base of the lake, and they will feed into a geothermal heat-pump. There are various forms of geothermal heating, but, in its own way, it is basically like a heat-pump. Once the hot water comes through the conditioning unit, it will be stored in 500-litre storage tanks in the plant room. A normal household has a 180-litre tank. Then that stored heat will be piped through all floors on both levels, and also into radiators in the upstairs bedrooms.

This wonderful passive thermal store, once it comes up to temperature, will have the ability to maintain a very constant heat all year round with very little heat input. The open fireplaces are more for aesthetics and atmosphere than for the control of the day-to-day temperature in the house. There is a significant cost in the installation of the system, but once it is established we will be able to heat the castle virtually for the cost of running a couple of freezers. Dot and Neil will get payback on the installation cost within five years, and then the castle will be self-sufficient so far as heating is concerned.

The most important thing for me is that it embodies all the principles I hold in terms of thermal mass, passive heat and also the chance to use a geothermal system. This is my first system being done in a lake, but I have

Construction of the
secret passage that leads
to the dungeon.

The not-so-secret
secret passage.

designed three in-ground geothermal systems, so it is starting to happen a lot more.

Water for the castle will come from the bore that supplies the farm and restaurant, and we have a very effective sewerage disposal system. Because we are on an island, we have to be able to get our waste off. Normal sewage runs into a 100-mm or 110-mm diameter pipe down into the main sewers. In our case we are going to macerate the sewage in a storage tank, and then it will be pumped off the island through a 50-mm macerating pump to effluent treatment tanks, and dosed into a dispersal field located in one of the paddocks to the south. By the time it gets into that system, it will have broken down to a point where the treated discharge can be safely dispersed into the ground.

But enough about heating systems and waste disposal! The eight turrets will be a more charming feature of the castle. The builders have made up an inspired piece of formwork — a hinged shutter that looks like a giant, round cake tin a third of the height of the towers. It is another example of the ingenuity of these local guys. 'Right,' they say, 'what's a way that we can make this happen?'

Most of the turrets are functional rather than purely decorative. The first is Dot's potting shed, and that is accessible only from outside the castle. The second will be used as a wood shed and can be accessed from the garage or from the outside. They will be just a little taller than one storey, with a high ceiling and beautiful detailing around the top. All of the turrets on the top floor are integrated into the floor plan of the bedrooms and project out over the side of the building. Guests will be able to sit there and take in the view through the arrow slit windows.

Obtaining the resource consent and building permit was a lengthy process that went on for nearly three years. The plans were completed and we applied to the

Waitaki District Council (WDC) for a resource consent in November 2010, and a year into the process we seemed no further ahead. I have been dealing with district councils for more than 25 years through both their resource management regulatory services and their building consent services, and have handled some extremely large resource consent applications in a lot of sensitive landscape areas, so I am well aware of the processes and the level of documentation required.

In fact I would stake my reputation on the standard of the documentation we presented to the WDC over and over again. But in 25 years of dealing with such projects with Queenstown Lakes District and other major councils around the country, including Auckland (Rodney) in recent years, I have never faced such a long, drawn-out processing of an application.

In addition, it is very important that everyone understands that, contrary to a statement published in an article in *The Press* on Saturday, 21 December 2013, the New Zealand Transport Agency is *not* building and paying for the north-bound and south-bound access lanes from State Highway 1 into the Riverstone complex. Dot and Neil are paying hundreds of thousands of dollars to build the intersection. My traffic engineer commented that it will be the best intersection on the state highway between Christchurch and Bluff. In my opinion, Transit New Zealand have made this an extremely difficult and costly exercise by insisting that Neil and Dot comply with every single tiny regulation they could find. By contrast KiwiRail, Network Waitaki and Fulton Hogan could not have been more helpful in proceeding with the project.

While waiting for the resource consent, Neil decided to start work on the lake. The 4-ha paddock in front of the restaurant had always been a soggy piece of land. There was an iron pan beneath the topsoil, so the water wasn't easily dispersed into the water table and the paddock was choked with rushes. We decided to locate the island as far south as possible on the lake, to make sure the restaurant still had a view of the mountains while avoiding having to pull down trees and encroach on the next paddock.

The men from Rooney Earthmoving surveyed the site and brought in two huge motor-scraper Caterpillars. When Sarah and I stood beside them, our heads didn't come up to the top of the wheels. Sometimes they had to use three machines, but even these big Cats had trouble and had to push one another through the iron pan. The scrapers worked non-stop for about three months, digging the gravel from the 45-ha lake to a depth of 3 m. We stockpiled the topsoil in a heap that stood half the height of the fully grown trees at the south side of the paddock, and supplied the gravel to the Oamaru shingle suppliers located six minutes south of the farm. This meant we didn't have mountains of unwanted gravel on our property, and they had a year's supply they didn't have to dig for on their own site.

Once we had excavated the hole, we had to line it with three layers of topsoil to hold the water in. The men spread the first layer, got the water tankers in to soak it, then rolled it over and over again with a vibrating roller, repeating the process and putting seepage plugs down each time to check the volume and rate of the seepage in a 24-hour period. Once the seal was established, the entire lake was lined with gravel and rolled again several times to prevent the soil from washing away.

It has been designed as a working lake, filled with excess water from our irrigation allocation. Neil can use it for irrigating the paddocks when the season gets dry, and then top it up when we have an excess of water again. As for populating the lake, we'll go to Fish and Game to see what they advise, but Neil thinks that the eels will come in naturally as fingerlings. Once the lake is full, after we have completed building the castle and laying out the heating pipework, I will landscape the banks with native plants, but I can't have anything where the roots go down and cause seepage, so whatever I do has to be pretty seriously thought out.

It will be great fun for our grandkids in kayaks, but at this point we don't plan to open the lake to the public, although they will be able to stroll around it on a boardwalk. We have already built a big jetty, and you can walk out there from the restaurant. It faces the mountains, and even now, when the castle is less than half-built, you can see the reflection in the water. I can't wait to see it fully constructed. It will be spectacular with its towers and castellations.

Neil and I didn't know anything about the building industry when we started this project, so there was a lot of to-ing and fro-ing when we had to make the decision about the construction materials. At first we looked at the possibility of building the castle in big tilt-slab concrete panels. We went to different manufacturers and learnt that it is possible to put any number of different finishes on the concrete, but in the end I couldn't see a castle just being pushed up in slabs. I believed it had to be built properly from ground level up, as it would have been centuries ago. And while Neil wasn't too concerned about any historical significance, he wanted to be sure it would be a solid construction. We considered using Oamaru stone, but the cost of the reinforcement needed to meet the building regulations ruled that out, so we settled on the masonry blocks with an Oamaru stone veneer.

Three years had gone past since we had confirmed the design, and in that time the builder we had originally engaged was that much older and didn't want to take on what amounted to a large commercial project. He got a big building company to put together a fixed-price contract, and when we saw the full extent of what we would be up for, it was more than we could afford. And that was the point at which everything ground to a halt, until a local businessman, Alan McLay stepped in and said, 'We can do this! Let's put together a local team.'

Alan came with us to see Jim Hannan, who had been a senior building inspector for the Waitaki District Council for many years. We asked Jim if he thought he could organise a team of people he believed could work on a job like ours. We explained that the build might take two or even three years of sporadic work, and that the tradespeople would have to be prepared to come when they were needed on a straight labour-only contract.

Jim agreed to act as project manager, and gave us a list of the people in the town whom he thought had the skill and the stickability to build the house we wanted. When we invited everyone to a meeting on 13 August 2012 in the conservatory at home, some of the tradespeople expressed concerns that the building was going to take so long that they would not be able to continue building for other people at the same time. We worked out that if we had only one builder and an apprentice, we could get this enormous house built in the simplest and most cost-effective way over a much longer period of time.

It has been lucky for us that we have found an absolute gem of a builder in Michael Spiers. He came on board as the chief builder, with a small team of people he can bring onto the site when he needs extra help. In the meantime, Jason Anderson turned up. His parents had worked for us on the dairy farms at different times, so we had known him for most of his life. Jason had been working in the mines in Australia, and had spent time in the New Zealand Army serving in Afghanistan. Now he wanted to return to Oamaru, so he asked Neil for a job.

But Neil knew Jason wouldn't be making as much money on a dairy farm as he would do in the mines, and he kept trying to put him off. That didn't stop Jason, who kept on ringing, and in the end Neil said, 'I'll give you a job on the building site, Jason, but you might as well take on a builder's apprenticeship so you have got something worthwhile out of it at the end of the project.' So Jason is on the farm payroll and doing his apprenticeship with Michael on the building site. They get on very well, and together have done an amazing job.

Sarah is still just as involved in the project as she was in the design phase, and she has her own take on the way the building is progressing.

I work in Wanaka with some of the top-end builders doing highly technical, skilled architectural work, so I am used to working with a very high calibre of tradesperson. And I am just blown away, because I am getting that calibre of tradespeople here in Oamaru. I could never have imagined that I would have got such an amazing crew. Michael Spiers is inspiring as a builder, because of his attention to detail. Just as importantly, he and I have the perfect working relationship, and that doesn't always happen between an architect and a builder. We talk to each other every week. Dot's the boss, but when it comes to detailing, he always rings me and says, 'I think we could do this' and 'Is this how you want it?'

If it is an aesthetic thing I always talk to Dot first, but if it is a straight building issue I handle it with Mike. The same with the sparkies and the plumber. This is a project on a scale that would normally be handled by a big professional construction company, and to try and build it with a group of local tradespeople is pretty mind-boggling. Jim Hannan is doing a wonderful job of running the project, but the guys on the site are just to die for. We have got two separate electrical companies working together. We have got builders from various different little private companies and practices. Ian Gold and his team of blockies — the people doing the concrete

Sarah Scott, Dot and
Mike Spiers — what a
formidable team!

Second floor concrete pour —
all hands on deck.

masonry — are also applying the Oamaru stone veneer.

Everybody has risen to the challenge, and I put that down to the sheer personality of the Smiths. They show so much respect for, and get on so well with, all the trades-people that everyone wants to do their level best for Neil and Dot. Every single tradesperson working on it is doing so with a huge amount of pride and care and satisfaction in their work that is shown in every aspect of the project. The quality of the work, the attention to detail — I am just so proud of those guys, and I consider myself privileged to be working with them.

Before we started the physical construction we took Alan McLay's advice and made two trips with him to the massive Yiwu builders' wholesale markets in China to see a wider range of product choices. My role, in terms of the China trips, is to assess the quality of the items we need and make sure they comply with the New Zealand building code. Contrary to local legend, the castle is not being built out of China. First and foremost, Neil and Dot are using as much local input as they can, and certainly anything that has a structural or load-bearing function comes from building suppliers in New Zealand.

Alan has business interests in China and was able to arrange an agent, an interpreter and a driver, who were essential, because even seasoned business people who have spent years sourcing supplies out of Yiwu would never be able to find what they needed among the thousands of outlets.

I have worked with our engineer, Tim Bradford of Lewis Bradford in Christchurch, for about 20 years and have enormous respect for his professionalism. Part of what makes him so good at his work is his cautious approach to a building project, and he was more than a little ambivalent about sourcing building supplies out of China. While I wasn't making the assumption that all Chinese products were made on the cheap, I have to say that on the first trip I was probably leaning more towards Tim's view.

Once we had got there and had been shown around by the professionals in Alan's import company, I could see that what was available ranged from rubbish to the peak of superior quality. In every instance, when it came to ordering materials, Neil and Dot deferred to my professional knowledge. The products Dot is looking for are purely decorative. For example, she would like to design a family crest and have it made in marble for the floor in the atrium.

We were rigorous in the design of the castle to make sure that the entire building worked to block modules. That is because every time a block-layer has to stop and cut another concrete block, it slows things down and adds to the time cost. We have designed and drawn the plans so that even all the window and door openings are block modules. And the care we took in the drawing process to build in those economies is having a triple-fold payback in the way the construction has proceeded.

The building project was due to start just after we returned from our second trip to China, so we brought back a large quantity of fully coated 18-mm thick marine plywood, which we have used everywhere on the construction site. Mike and Jason boxed the foundations immaculately using this beautiful plywood as their formwork. And when Ian Gold came to lay the blocks, the foundations that he started from were all perfect to the block modules within 1–2 mm, so that once they started laying, it went like clockwork.

It is only fair to say that Ian was less than enthusiastic about coming on board with the build, because he thought he was going to be trapped in the castle for years. However, he was able to lay the blocks for the first stage, then go off and do another five houses and come back for a while. He has relaxed and realised that in fact he can do it without compromising his work on other projects. It is a daunting project for everyone involved, even an experienced builder who has done a lot of big houses — nothing could compare to this.

There are just two builders working on the castle year round, and I thought they should have their say on the way the project has been shaping up, so here's a bit of a chat with the builders, Mike Spiers and Jason Anderson:

Mike: Jim Hannan, the project manager, told me about this big job he had tried to get through council for the past couple of years, and they took me and Fraser Nelson on to do the building work. We worked together for a while with a couple of others. No one was the boss. Some of us are good at some aspects of building, and some of us are good at others. Then Jason came on as the apprentice, so there's just the two of us now, except when we need to bring in the blockies and the guys on the concrete pump.

At other times we bring in extra builders like Fraser and Jeff Simpson. They work on the concrete floors and things like that. Fraser has done a lot of concreting, so he can screed and we all finish it off together. When the blockies are working here and the concrete pourers, Jase and I are marking everything out for them — tying all the steel and double-checking to make sure everything is correct.

This building is like nothing I have worked on before. With a normal house, the builder just looks at the plan and builds the house, then gets the council inspections and other paperwork, and at the end of the job he gets a code of compliance. Here, on this job, it is so involved and uses so much steelwork that we are working closely with the engineer. We are constantly looking at plans and getting him to sign off different parts of the steelwork and structural elements.

Jason: We do all the physical work, too. Formwork. Reinforcing. Concreting. There's all the turrets that have to be made. We have done everything on-site by hand instead of getting things pre-made.

Mike: We started working on the site in September 2012, but I had to take a couple of weeks off to go and finish one of my subdivisions. We don't know how long we will be on this job. We are in the first week of December 2013 now, so it will take another year at least. Probably a bit more.

Jason: This is the first real building I have been on, and just trying to get your head around the plans is pretty challenging. It would be challenging even for a qualified builder, let alone an apprentice. Every decision you make is critical. If it's not right, then the next step is going to turn to custard, so it is a huge challenge and you are constantly thinking out of the square.

Mike: Jase is going to learn a lot as an apprentice on this one job because he's working one-to-one with me — a qualified builder. He's going to be good at reading and understanding plans. He's going to be very good at formwork and reinforcing.

Jason: We have had a few adventures and funny incidents in the last year or so. A couple of days ago, just before we knocked off work, we turned around and saw a magpie land right up the top.

Mike: I said, 'Jase, look at that magpie. Look how close it is.' And we were joking around, saying, 'Come here, boy. Come here, boy', and the thing flew up to us and landed on Jason, who held hold of it while I took photos.

Jason: It landed on the toe of my work boot, and then after a few minutes he flew away. The next day we were up here for about an hour, and he turned up again. We were patting him and gave him a pancake with some jam on it. We had to hand-feed it to him, but the gardener, Leigh, took it home as a family pet to release when it is old enough to survive in the wild.

Mike: We named him Fraser, because Fraser flies in and out. You hardly ever see him. But when he turns up now, we call him Magpie. And there was that other bit of excitement when a wall blew down in a hundred-year storm. Everyone was running around trying to hold it up, and it was quite a drama for a while, but we repaired the damage in no time. Dot was pretty upset, but she got over it after the shock had passed. She and Neil are fantastic. They are great to work for. Always positive. And I'll tell you what — Dot's good at cooking scones. I'm going to try and get the recipe off her. They're magic.

Jason: With her home-made jam. Ten out of ten. And she always wears a pink jumper so we can spot her when she arrives with them.

After the construction phase had begun in September 2012, I began to see design elements that needed to be changed. I rang Sarah and suggested that we could take out the garage doors at the back of the building, and add another tower to balance out the tower on the other side. While we were at it, we relocated the laundry into the garage, and created a more welcoming wheelchair access. The design is still evolving in smaller ways, because, as the construction advances, I can see elements that are not obvious when you see them on paper or the computer screen.

After the construction had been underway for eight or nine months, and once the walls started to go up, I told Sarah that I wasn't sure about using a flat stone veneer. I wanted to take a close look at some of the gracious old buildings around Oamaru to see how they had achieved the effect that made people admire them so much. She and I visited the Hall of

Memories at Waitaki Boys' High School and St Luke's church, where all the finishes to the bottom of door arches and window frames were made from big bolstered stones. You can see the marks on the stone from the chisels.

When I first started talking about building the castle, Bevan didn't take me seriously, but when Neil and I decided to go ahead with it, on the farm, he said to me, 'If you're going to do it, don't make a fake one. Make a real one that will be standing in 200 or 300 years.'

Thinking about that as we stood looking at those chisel marks, I said to Sarah, 'That tells you the history of the stone. It just makes you feel that your building is something substantial. It has got a better look. There is just such a difference between the plain and the bolstered look.'

So we went back out to the quarry and said to the manager, Bob Wilson, 'We want to have a look at the stones. What do you think about having them bolstered?' Bob was rapt! He said it would give us a magnificent texture and depth to the stone on the outside of the castle. Of course, it is a lot more work for the quarry people. But it will be worth it.

Pumping concrete to fill the
concrete blocks on the back
wall of the castle.

Pukeuri House and garden.

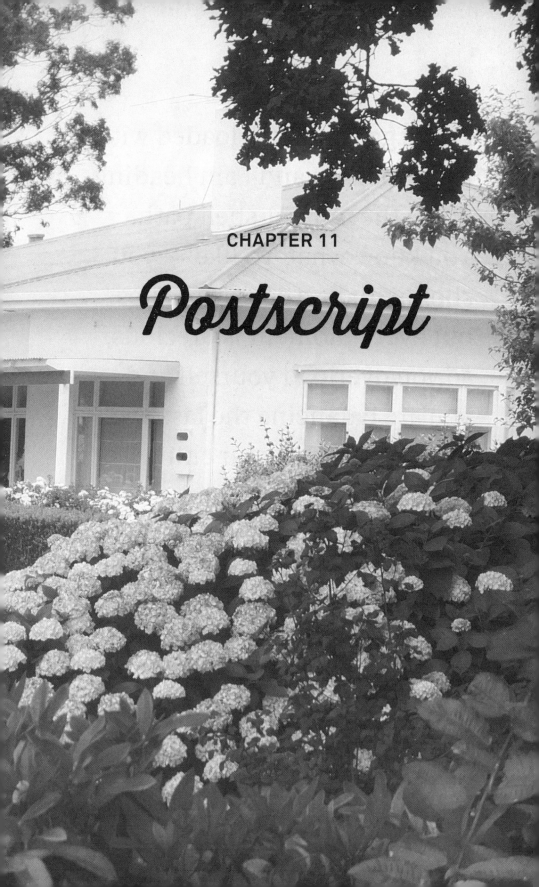

CHAPTER 11

Postscript

I have got my arms loaded with five cabbages and I am heading down the mussel-shell path. You know what it's like — you should make a couple of trips, but every moment is precious, so you overload yourself and you are balancing the last two cabbages under your chin. When I arrive at the end of the path, a car pulls up and a lady jumps out. 'Hi! I'm Melanie. You must be Dot.'

'Yes?'

'I really like that shot — can you do it again?'

Hell's teeth! I had only just made it this time, let alone going back and doing it again. The camera man jumps out of the car and I stand there, balancing tumbling cabbages while George gets himself ready.

'OK. Ready to roll. No! Go back again, and I want you to

come out of the garden beside those red poppies this time.'

I duck back into the garden again and walk out onto the path, cabbages dropping from my arms.

'Uh-oh. Better do that again.'

I load the rolling cabbages into my arms again, and get them balanced well enough to be able to walk back towards the camera. It lacks a certain spontaneity, but — it's a take. My introduction to being a TV star. I thought, 'This is going to be a long day.' If you are a proper TV star you get a make-up artist, a wardrobe designer, a set dresser. How come I got none of these? It's just 'here we are, and let's get shooting'.

'What are we going to shoot?' I ask. Melanie has obviously been well-briefed by the person who put her onto me in the first place. She says, 'We'll start at Pukeuri where you have all the furniture and things you have been collecting for the castle. We'll start the story there.'

I jump into my trusty blue ute, and the TV team follow me in a cloud of gravelly dust. I have never done anything like this before. I am usually the one taking the photographs and am never in them, so it is a new experience to have a camera follow me wherever I go. Melanie and her director, Keith, take a quick tour around my restored villa full of collections from around the world — the African room, the Chinese room, my kitchen full of Portuguese cabbage-ware china, the bedrooms. They talk about how they are going to proceed and the plan is set. Keith says, 'I want the two of you to walk down the hall towards the camera.' Mel is asking the questions and I'm saying whatever comes into my head. It's so easy!

We go into the dining room. They tell me what I have to do. I look at the table setting and realise I have forgotten to polish the silver. This time it is me who is calling, 'Stop!' Mel and I get cracking and whip around the table settings with soft cloths and a tin of Silvo, then off we go again, with Melanie asking the questions and me answering, while Keith sits in a chair off-camera, overseeing the proceedings. Then they are off out to the farm to interview the men, and I rush home to feed the chooks and talk to sales reps for the shop. Just another busy day.

The phone had rung one night in April 2012. 'Hello, Dot. Melanie Reid calling from TV3's *Third Degree* programme. I have been given your name as someone who might agree to feature in a documentary. We are looking for a positive story to inspire people instead of all the negative stuff we have to report on. What do you think?'

Long silence at my end. For the first time in my life, I was speechless. When I had recovered, I said, 'Us? What on earth will we talk about? I have got nothing special to say. We are just who we are — nothing out of the ordinary. We are just like everyone else we know.'

I could hear the smile in Melanie's voice. 'I have been told, Dot, that you're a bit of a hard-case and could cope with us doing a story. We would like to do it on building the castle, the farming operation, the restaurant, the shop and the garden aspects that make up your business. And I have been told you have pink hair! What do you think?'

Another long silence.

'We'd really like to come down. Have a think about it and give me a call back. Cheers. Talk soon.'

I hung up the phone and turned to Neil. 'Guess what? TV3 wants to do a doco on the family.' The quiet, shy Neil just looked at me with a silly expression on his face. Many cups of tea later, he said, 'Give her a ring and say OK. It'll be good for Oamaru and put the district on the map again.'

Six months later, in the spring, the *Third Degree* team came back to Riverstone and we filmed another segment, this time focusing on the castle. We went over to the island and walked around the site with the plans. The building project has come a long way since when they were last here. Melanie interviews Bevan working in the restaurant kitchen, his older brother

Michael making silage out in the paddocks, and Neil in the cowshed with the cows — the source of our income and, after his family, the love of his life.

Winter came and we had not had word on when the programme would go to air. It had been so long since the filming that we put the whole episode to the back of our minds and went off on a trip to Africa. One morning, as we were going up to the restaurant for breakfast, Monique put a call through to Neil's cell phone. She was jumping out of her skin with excitement. 'TV3 aired the programme last night, and the whole place here has gone mad!'

Neil handed me the phone, and Monique was babbling so fast I could barely make out what she was saying. 'Dot, you won't believe the reaction we've had to the programme last night.' The restaurant had to put a staff member on the job of receiving all the phone calls from people ringing to congratulate us on what was obviously a very entertaining doco.

She said the emails were pouring in, with people offering all sorts of things for the castle. Someone wanted to sell us suits of armour, an elderly woman wanted to donate all her antique furniture. Other folk rang with business offers: furniture makers, an iron monger, joiners, a woman who makes fibrous plaster moulds for cornices, a kitchen designer, glass chandelier makers, and others with different products they thought we would like.

Not only that, but people were pouring into the restaurant in waves they hadn't seen since winning the award three years before. It was unbelievable! She said, 'We can't wait for you to get back home.'

Neil and I ate our breakfast with a funny look on our faces. What was *this* all about? We wondered how the programme had portrayed us. When TV3 left our property we had nothing more to do with the process, and it was up to their team in the studio to put the documentary together. We had no idea of the format, and wondered what it was that had got everyone so excited, but they had obviously done a good job judging by the response.

It would be three weeks before we could see it, so we simply got on with having our holiday in South Africa and Botswana's equally exciting Okavango Delta. I felt a little tingle of excitement whenever I thought about the programme, but then we would drive through a herd of elephants making their way to a waterhole, catch our first-ever sighting of a leopard lying in a tree, watch hyenas tearing at the dead carcass of an old elephant, and our TV fame disappeared to the back of my mind. Neil didn't say much about it.

As we were flying back home, the Air New Zealand hostess came up to us in the plane and said, 'Are you the Smiths? We watched your programme on the tele and loved it.' As we were walking through the airport, people smiled at us in a way I have never known before, and I thought, 'Gosh, all these people can't have watched the tele.' It's quite odd when strangers keep looking at you as though they know you and come up to say, 'Hello, Dot, Neil. We saw you on TV. It was a great show!' I was to hear this dozens of times a day in the next six months. It seems like the whole country watched the show that night.

Later, people got in touch to tell us how they had come to see the show. One Oamaru lady who doesn't have a TV said she was in her pyjamas and dressing gown when the next door neighbours rang and told her to come over quickly — Dot Smith was on tele. The neighbours were renovating their house, so the TV was in the bedroom and the two ladies and the man piled onto the bed and watched the doco together.

When we got home to Riverstone, our first priority was to have a good night's sleep after such a long flight. Michael invited us to come over to his place the next day, because he had recorded the programme. How strange it was to see ourselves looking out at us from the screen. In fact it was quite funny, and I sat there laughing at how they had put the little incidents together. I particularly liked the studio work where they had done 3D images of the castle structure from the plans. It was the first time I had seen how it will look, and I thought, 'No wonder everyone is excited about it.'

Apart from the two anchor men calling me 'slightly mad' and 'an eccentric millionaire' (obviously they had never met me) we thought it was a good programme. And the interest it has brought to Riverstone has been astounding. For weeks and months we had people coming to stand in front of the restaurant so that they could see the progress of the castle construction and to meet the lady with the pink hair. We even had people flying down from Auckland to see the castle and eat at the restaurant.

Monique and Bevan have found that the show has increased their restaurant bookings and created a new kind of customer — known as 'the castle fans'. People still ask the restaurant staff where they can find Dot. Some have asked if I will meet them while they are having dinner so they can introduce me to their mothers! The most frequently asked questions we have to field are: Will it have a drawbridge? Does it have a dungeon? And: When will it be finished? I would never have imagined the interest the show would bring. It was entertaining, but also told the story of an ordinary everyday Kiwi family and the hard work that is bringing my lifetime dream to fruition. I always say to people: 'Follow your dream. You only come to this world once.'

A couple of months after the TV programme went to air, there came a phone call from Random House publishing company. Would I consider writing a book? Again, I had to say, 'Goodness! Whatever would I write about?'

They said, 'Just be yourself and write about who you are, where you came from and the journey that has brought you to where you are today.'

What a subject!

Random House said there was a writer here in Oamaru who could help me put it together, and she has certainly made my job so much easier. We have had a very short time to write it, which is probably lucky in a way — otherwise, with more time, I could have unearthed a lot more information and the book would have been the size of an encyclopaedia.

Sometimes it has been quite an emotional experience, digging up all my locked-away memories, and by the end of a writing day I have felt more exhausted than after a day hauling weeds out of the garden. Sometimes it has been hilarious as memories of funny incidents have come flooding back. And I have remembered and thought about things that I would never write about.

I know this story will bring back memories to readers who have had a similar upbringing to mine. 'We did that! I remember that!' Or it will inspire people to do whatever it takes to make their dream come true. I hope it does that for you.

Remember — girls can do anything.

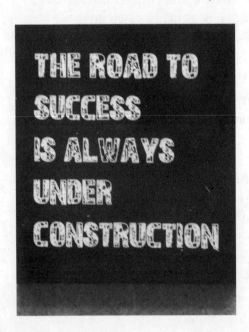

THE ROAD TO SUCCESS IS ALWAYS UNDER CONSTRUCTION

Acknowledgements

To Random House for giving me the opportunity to write this book, and to Barbara Larson for her encouragement and for having the confidence to let me loose!

Thanks too, to the team at Random House — it hasn't been easy to contain me — a job well done!

To Nathalie Brown — thank you. We met as strangers and finished as friends. It's been wonderful working with you while pulling the story together.

To Neil — sorry about all the meals of eggs on toast when I ran out of time to cook.

To my family for their support in lots of little ways.

To Sarah Scott and staff — what can I say? Without you my dream would never have come true.

To Mike Spiers, Jason Anderson, Ian Gold and their workers. You are the greatest of dream teams.

To my shop staff and gardeners for keeping everything on track while I wandered off to work on this book.

Thank you to Fiona Andersen for her gorgeous photographs.

For more information about our titles please go to
www.randomhouse.co.nz